THE FUTURE BATTLEFIELD
AND THE
ARAB-ISRAELI CONFLICT

The Near East Policy Series is a joint project of Transaction Publishers and The Washington Institute for Near East Policy, a private, educational foundation supporting scholarly research and informed debate on U.S. interests in the Near East.

THE FUTURE BATTLEFIELD AND THE ARAB-ISRAELI CONFLICT

Hirsh Goodman
W. Seth Carus

Transaction Publishers
New Brunswick (U.S.A.) and London (U.K.)

Library of Congress Catalog Number: 89-20245
ISBN: 0-88738-318-1 (cloth); 0-88738-822-1 (paper)
Printed in the United States of America

Library of Congress Cataloging-in-Publication Data

Goodman, Hirsh.
    The future battlefield and the Arab-Israeli Conflict/Hirsh
Goodman, W. Seth Carus.
      p. cm. -- (The Near East policy series: 1)
    ISBN 0-88738-318-1. -- ISBN 0-88738-822-1 (pbk.)
    1. Israel-Arab conflicts. 2. Israel--Armed Forces--Weapons
systems. 3. Arab countries--Armed Forces--Weapons systems.
I. Carus, W. Seth. II. Title. III. Series.
DS119.7.G644   1989
956.04--dc20
                                 89-20245
                                      CIP

TABLE OF CONTENTS

Appendix, Glossary, Index, and Tables

Acknowledgements

This book was made possible by the encouragement and support of The Washington Institute for Near East Policy. Martin Indyk and the staff of the institute provided a home for the authors while the manuscript was being written. Without their assistance, this book would not have been published.

Many people took the time to talk to the authors. Unfortunately, circumstances make it impossible to acknowledge everyone to whom a debt is owed. Thanks are due Ze'ev Schiff, Edward N. Luttwak, Stephen P. Glick, Joseph Bermudez, Jr., and the organizers and participants in the conference on the future battlefield organized by the Jaffee Center for Strategic Studies. The authors are indebted to Ronnie Hope for his careful edit of the manuscript. The errors that remain are the sole responsibility of the authors.

Hirsh Goodman
W. Seth Carus

1: The Strategic Context of the Future Arab-Israeli Battlefield

A revolution in the technology of war is now taking place that will radically change the manner in which battles will be fought in the future. The new technologies are a direct result of the rapid pace of both military and civilian scientific innovation. In numerous fields, fundamental advances are making possible the development of new devices, enhancing the performance of existing systems, and making economical the production of systems that in the past were impossible or too difficult and costly to produce. New options for military hardware will become available with growing rapidity. In the coming decade, the battlefield will be filled with new types of sensors, increasingly capable command, control and communications (C^3) systems, and more accurate and deadly munitions.

These devices will have an influence on virtually every aspect of warfare, from the mundane to the esoteric, and, as a result, the battlefield of the 1990s will be considerably different from anything we have known to date, both in terms of offensive capabilities and defensive answers. In some cases, sophisticated military systems that worked well only a few years ago may no longer be effective. Similarly, innovative new tactics and operational methods will become possible through the creative exploitation of the capabilities of new military equipment. In turn, this will transform military doctrine at the tactical, operational and strategic levels.

The tools of war have always influenced the character of wars. In the past, the appearance of new forms of communication (the telegraph, the radio), transportation (steam ships, the railroad, the aircraft), and new weapons (the long bow, gunpowder weapons, the machinegun, the tank, the missile) have all fundamentally transformed warfare. What distinguishes the current revolution is the rapidity with which new technological developments are taking place, and the broad range of technologies that are contributing to the transformation.[1]

This military-technical revolution will have significant implications for Israel and for its potential Arab adversaries. New types of military equipment will enter service in the region, both through the import of systems built elsewhere and through local development. The next war is not going to be won by the side that possesses the better technical array of systems, but by the side that best knows how to integrate them into its overall conduct of war.

Common wisdom attributes the successes of Israeli military forces over more numerous and sometimes better equipped Arab opponents to the superior quality of Israeli equipment. After the Israeli air force decimated the Syrian air force and air defense forces

---

[1] The Appendix provides a more detailed discussion of the new technologies, along with an examination of some of the new types of military systems that are becoming available.

in the Bekaa in 1982, it was asserted, only half facetiously, that the outcome would have been much the same even if the two sides had exchanged weapons (Israel operating Syria's Soviet-supplied equipment; the Syrians Israel's modern Western systems).

This comment is only partly correct. Although wars are ultimately decided by the people who fight them, to attribute victory or defeat to manpower alone, or to the quality of weapons alone, is false. To do so reflects a fundamental misunderstanding of the critical interactions between technology and military institutions that have developed as weapons have become more sophisticated.

Had Israel indeed possessed an arsenal of Soviet equipment, these weapons would have been quickly modified and upgraded in a myriad of ways. The propensity of the Israeli military to continually modify its equipment is not merely an interesting sidelight, but rather an essential component of Israel's qualitative superiority. It demonstrates an appreciation that weapons, like any tools, work best if they are tailored to the particular tasks at hand.

Such qualitative considerations will remain central to an understanding of the Arab-Israeli military balance, since the quantitative aspects of the conflict in the future will not differ dramatically from those of today. There will be no major expansion in the size of the arsenals of the countries in the region, and as a result the most important changes will be mainly qualitative, not quantitative. This emphasizes a critical truism – that it is not the quantities of weapons that will decide the future balance of power equation in the Middle East, but rather the quality of the weapons, the mix of weapons held by each military force, and the ability of the armed forces of the countries to use them.

Crucial, as well, are the new time-frames these

technologies will create. Increasingly, governments – including those at the superpower level – are going to find themselves having to articulate quick responses to complex and dangerous situations against constantly diminishing time-frames.

Any accurate assessment of impact of the new technologies also requires an understanding of the regional context. Hence it is necessary both to evaluate the impact of the new technologies and to examine the regional strategic environment expected to exist in the 1990s.

The Strategic Environment

In early 1989, Syria continues to be intractably hostile to Israel; Iraq and Iran have accepted a ceasefire but are rearming in case hostilities resume; Israel and Egypt are at peace; and a state of *de facto* non-belligerency exists between Jordan and Israel. These realities have isolated Syria within the Arab world and have resulted in the creation of a strategic environment not conducive to the initiation of a major war against Israel. Nevertheless, wider Arab participation will be possible if strategic realities change dramatically in the coming years.

The state of peace between Israel and Egypt is likely to continue, even if today's formal agreements degenerate into tacit non-belligerency due to some unforeseen change in either Egyptian policy or leadership. From a purely military point of view, the breakdown of peace with Egypt will not have an immediate impact on Israel, although it could force Israel to increase the size of the forces assigned to the Egyptian frontier. The security arrangements included in the Camp David accords provide Israel with adequate early warning to organize diplomatic and military responses.[2] Moreover, even under the current arrangements, the Sinai desert provides a 250 kilometer deep zone that separates Israel from a potentially hostile Egyptian army, adding a physical buffer to the constraints already in place and further diminishing the immediacy of the threat.

Jordan, as long as the Hashemites are in power, will remain in a state of quasi-non-belligerency with Israel, whether or not there is progress on the Palestinian question. When, and if, the Iran-Iraq war ends, Jordan's strategic posture will change, but it is highly doubtful that King Hussein, or his successors, will take Jordan out of the Western sphere of influence or into military conflict with Israel over issues that are tangential to broad Jordanian national interests. Israel has a long and exposed border with Jordan, but so long as the Jordanians refuse to allow their territory to be used as a base for attacks on Israel, any Arab offensive will be geographically limited in a fashion that will make defensive responses easier to organize.

As long as the Iran-Iraq war continued, the Iraqi military was not able to take part in a war with Israel. This removed the largest military force in the Arab world from the ranks of the confrontation states. Even now Iraq is concerned primarily with the threat from Iran. It will take time for it to rebuild its military and revive its economy, and it is likely that Iraq will withdraw from involvement in the Arab-Israeli dispute in favor of national reconstruction. It

---

[2] The Camp David agreement limits the size of Egyptian forces permanently stationed in the Sinai, as well as the amount of infrastructure that can be built there. It also provides geographic constraints, essentially limiting the Egyptians to the western third of the Sinai.

also is not evident that the Iraqis would willingly participate in a war against Israel even if they were able. Relations between Iraq and Syria have been strained since the late 1970s, and Syrian support for Iran since the start of the Gulf War makes it doubtful that an Iraq ruled by President Saddam Husayn would take any steps to benefit the Syrians.

The Iran-Iraq war, and a variety of associated political-military consequences, also have limited the ability of Gulf states like Saudi Arabia and Kuwait to participate in a war with Israel. From a military point of view, Iranian strikes against Saudi shipping and the prospect of direct Iranian attacks on Saudi territory have made it difficult for the Saudis to commit forces to fight Israel. However the war develops, the Gulf states will have to assign a high priority to defense against Iran. Politically, the evident dependence of the Gulf states on the United States for security assistance and the renewal of diplomatic relations with Egypt despite its peace treaty with Israel make it less likely that these countries would align themselves with Syria in an anti-Israel military coalition.

The Lebanese border will continue to pose tactical problems for Israel in the conduct of counter-terrorism activities. However, even though terrorism will remain an endemic problem in Lebanon, and internationally, it will not pose a threat to Israel's existence.

These realities have combined to tilt the balance of military power to Israel's advantage. By early 1986, Israeli military planners had come to believe that this situation would continue, and that there was little immediate chance of a new anti-Israel military alliance emerging in the near future.[3] It appears that

---

[3] As an example of this focus, in early 1986 a senior Israeli military official stated that Israeli military planning for the

this view was shared in Damascus.[4] Consequently, from Israel's point of view, the second half of the 1980s emerged as a period of strategic stability.

Nevertheless, it should be recognized that these fundamental conditions could change rapidly. The strategic environment in the 1990s could be very different from the one prevailing now, and depending on the nature of the changes, it is possible that

---

next year would be grounded on four basic assumptions:

> 1. No comprehensive war with an Arab coalition is expected in 1986.

> 2. There is only a small chance of a major war with Syria, but there is a chance of a deterioration.

> 3. Israel must prepare itself for the prospect of a war with Syria in 1986.

> 4. There is a possibility of political changes toward the creation of Arab coalitions in 1986.

This is a paraphrase of the comments of Major General Dan Shomron, then Deputy Chief of Staff of the Israeli Defense Forces, quoted by *Jerusalem Domestic Service*, April 2, 1986, as translated in Foreign Broadcast Information Service (FBIS), *Daily Report: Middle East and Africa*, April 3, 1986, p. I2.

[4] Note the following exchange in a 1986 interview of Syrian Defense Minister Mustafa Talas in *Der Spiegel*:

> Question: You would only dare to begin the war against Israel if Iraq and Iran were on your side.

> Response: Correct, but such an alliance will come into existence only when Saddam Husayn is gone.

Der Spiegel, September 22, 1986, as translated in FBIS, *Daily Report: Middle East and Africa*, September 23, 1986, pp. H4-H5.

countries besides Syria might participate in a future Arab-Israeli war. The recent history of the conflict strongly indicates that relationships within the Arab world can quickly undergo fundamental transformations, and alliances can shift in unexpected ways.[5] As rapidly changing conditions in the Persian Gulf in the summer of 1987 demonstrated, the Middle East can be highly unstable, and the strategic realities of today can be overtaken by unexpected developments.

Supplementary and External Force Factors

The issue of possible alignments in the Arab world is complicated and remains the source of serious internal argument within Israel's defense community. Views on the parameters of external force participation vary widely. This disparity of views has an impact on all levels of military thinking, since the conclusions adopted will affect the size of the future Israeli army, the ratio of standing forces to reserve units, the nature of weapons development, the composition of the forces, and strategic doctrines.

Israel's concerns are a direct function of the capabilities of the potential expeditionary forces. Even though certain countries might be unlikely to participate in a war, if they do their activities could seriously complicate Israeli military operations. For reasons that are only partially related to the Arab-Israeli conflict, the Saudi military has taken steps to ensure that its forces have a large degree of strategic

---

[5] For a survey of Arab military alliances aimed at Israel, see Hirsh Goodman, *Israel's Strategic Reality: The Impact of the Arms Race* (Washington, D.C.: The Washington Institute for Near East Policy, 1985), pp. 9-11.

mobility. Thus, they could be involved in hostilities relatively soon after a political decision in Riyadh to take part in a conflict. C-130 tactical transports and Boeing 747 transport jets have provided the Saudis with a strategic air lift capability. Saudi ground-attack F-5 squadrons have been trained and equipped for rapid redeployment. The combination of F-15 fighters and AWACS early-warning aircraft give the Saudis unique air-combat capabilities that could have a substantial impact in Arab military operations against Israel. The Saudis could also enhance Syria's arsenal with a sophisticated range of munitions, such as antitank weapons, sophisticated air-to-ground ordnance, and anti-aircraft weaponry (including Stinger missiles).

If the Iran-Iraq war comes to a negotiated end, it might make it possible for the Iraqis to contribute battle-trained, battle-disciplined military forces in very short order. Iraq currently has the largest military force in the Arab world, including 600,000 regulars, 480,000 reservists, and 650,000 in the Popular Army. Its air force has nearly 600 combat aircraft and its army has at least 5,000 battle tanks. An inventory of 2,800 tank transporters allows the Iraqis to quickly shift mechanized divisions from one area to another.[6] Even if the Iraqi military were reduced in size after the end of the war, Iraq could still play a major role in a conflict with Israel. Even though there are

---

[6] Aharon Levran and Zeev Eytan, *The Middle East Military Balance 1986* (Boulder, Colorado: Westview Press, 1987), pp. 251-258 for details of the Iraqi inventory. (This volume is the most recent edition of an annual study by the Jaffee Center for Strategic Studies at Tel Aviv University.) Israeli Defence Minister Yitzhak Rabin has claimed that Iraq had 6,000 tanks. See the transcript of his speech, "The U.S.S.R. in the Middle East: A Strategic Assessment," *Proceedings* of the Washington Institute for Near East Policy, July 2, 1987, p. 2.

reasons to believe that Iraq would be reluctant to participate in a war against Israel in the near term, the enhanced mobility of ground forces, its combat experience, and the improved quality of its hardware from both East and West, will make the Iraqis a potential problem for a long time.

The key element, from Israel's point of view, is one of timing. If wider Arab participation is planned before the opening stages of war, one can assume that the intelligence indicators of impending war will increase dramatically, allowing time for diplomatic and military responses to deter an outbreak of hostilities. If wider Arab participation is spontaneous and reactive to an initial attack by Syria alone, it will be less organized and less integrated and, as a result, less threatening. The longer a Syrian-Israeli war lasts, however, the greater the chances of such intervention, and even if used inefficiently, the addition of external forces would strain limited Israeli resources.

The appearance of expeditionary forces would demand ingenious and highly coordinated Israeli responses, spontaneous restructuring of operational priorities, and a deviation from pre-planned scenarios, thus complicating the task of sustaining a counterattack. An expansion of the conflict also could increase Israeli casualties and complicate the task of bringing hostilities to a quick end. But the longer the time lag between the outbreak of hostilities and the intervention of other Arab forces, the better Israel will be able to deal with such an expansion of the conflict. As time passes, Israel's call-up of reserves will provide more forces to deal with secondary fronts, and once an initial Syrian attack is blocked it should be possible to free force elements needed to stop the expeditionary forces.

Despite this possibility of wider intervention, for the purposes of this book it will be assumed that Israel's primary military adversary during the coming years is likely to be Syria. The coordinated participation of other Arab countries is unlikely, or will be extremely limited, posing at worst a tactical rather than a strategic concern for Israel. The opening and most crucial stages of a future war are most likely to take place along the Syrian-Israeli front with the Syrians relying only on their own forces. It is here that the impact of the new technologies will manifest itself. And it is here that the primary focus of the book rests.

In the course of this study, we will attempt to provide an answer to three critical questions:

> To what extent will the new technologies become available to Syria and Israel, and how will the systems impact on Syrian and Israeli military doctrines?

> How well will the new technologies be assimilated, and therefore what effect will they have on the Syrian-Israeli balance of military power?

> What impact will the new technologies have on strategic stability in the region, and especially on the effectiveness of deterrence?

The primary focus of this study will be the conventional battlefield. Terrorism, nuclear warfare, and chemical warfare will be considered only in passing. Although important topics, it is felt that to examine them would entail a diversion from the primary goal of this analysis, which is to highlight the implications of new technologies for the future Arab-Israeli battlefield.

2: The Syrian Dimension

Because Syria will be the central Arab participant in any Arab-Israeli war in the foreseeable future, conditions in Damascus will have a decisive impact on both the prospects of war and on its character, if it does erupt. Among the relevant factors will be the nature of the regime that rules Syria, the attitudes towards Israel of the group that holds power, and Syria's domestic political and economic situation.

Unfortunately, it is not easy to predict the future character of Syria's regime, given President Hafiz al-Asad's uncertain state of health and his seeming unwillingness to name a successor who could ensure an orderly transition of power. The stability of the regime has also been jeopardized by Syria's severe economic problems, which in 1987 caused a cabinet shake-up involving the replacement of the country's Prime Minister and twelve other ministers.[1] Not knowing the factional allegiance of Syria's

---

[1] David Butter, "Parliament probe leads to Syrian cabinet

future leadership, or its ideological persuasion, makes it possible only to speculate on Syria's ability to fight a war in the future or on its likely strategic agenda.

Nevertheless, the alternatives are limited and all of them bode poorly for those who would like to believe that Syria may adopt a more conciliatory posture in the future. Hafiz al-Asad might still be in power and, if not, elements of the Syrian political spectrum loyal to Asad and faithful to the Ba'ath party line may be in control. Alternatively, the country could be in the hands of a military dictatorship, or of the Sunni majority, or a constellation of minority factions. It could also be fragmented into sectarian areas of control. The attitudes of such groups towards the continuation of the Arab-Israeli conflict cannot be known with certainty, but there is no reason to suppose that they will differ fundamentally from those of the current regime. A fragmented Syria, preoccupied with internecine warfare, would be the least likely to initiate war with Israel, but it is also the most unlikely of the alternatives. Syria has had 17 years of relative stability under Asad and the instruments of state-control are firmly in place.

Syrian Strategic Thinking

The Syrians view Israel both as an artificial creation of world Zionism and as a tool used by an imperialist United States to dominate the Arab world.[2]   They believe that the ultimate objective is a

---

shake-up," *Middle East Economic Digest,* November 7, 1987, p. 42.

[2] Syrian attitudes towards Israel since the mid 1970s can be followed by examining the chapters on Syria in successive editions of the *Middle East Contemporary Survey,* published

Greater Israel. Hafiz al-Asad has said "We are convinced that Israel is seriously working to establish a state from the Nile to the Euphrates."[3] Despite Israel's power, the Syrians believe that it has fundamental weaknesses that will enable the Arabs to defeat it. Israel's dependence on American aid, its weak economy, the inherent justice of the Arab cause, and the willingness of the Arabs (under Syrian leadership) to continue the struggle despite heavy sacrifices all help ensure an ultimate Arab victory.[4] Just as it required centuries for the Arabs to finally expel the Crusaders from Palestine during the Middle Ages, so it might take a long time to defeat Israel. In the final analysis, the Syrians believe the conflict between Israel and the Arabs is between two irreconcilable cultures and, as such, can only be resolved by military means.[5]

This perspective of Israel has important strategic

---

annually by the Dayan Center of the Tel Aviv University. It is not hard to discover essentially similar statements in the Syrian media, as translated by the Foreign Broadcast Information Service (FBIS) in *Daily Report: Middle East and Africa*.

[3] *Damascus Television Service* in Arabic, February 18, 1986, as translated in FBIS, *Daily Report: Middle East and Africa*, February 19, 1986, p. H5.

[4] For typical examples, see the speech by Hafiz al-Asad in *Damascus Domestic Service* in Arabic, March 8, 1986, as translated in FBIS, *Daily Report: Middle East and Africa*, March 10, 1986, pp. H1-H3, and the interview with Asad read by *Damascus Domestic Service* in Arabic, January 24, 1987, as translated in FBIS, *Daily Report: Middle East and Africa*, January 28, 1987, pp. H1-H7.

[5] Yosef Olmert, "Whither Syria? The Politics of Dead Ends," a chapter to be included in a forthcoming book on Syria being prepared by the Washington Institute for Near East Policy.

implications. First, the Syrian conception of Israel leaves no obvious opening for a negotiated settlement to the conflict, since the dispute is seen as a fundamental struggle between an aggressive, illegitimate Israel and the rights of the Arab nation. Second, Israel's perceived expansionist goals make the creation of a deterrent designed to halt Israeli aggression against the Arab nation an essential short-term objective. Third, the concept that time works to the benefit of the Arab struggle reduces the importance of taking immediate action against Israel, and also reduces the significance of temporary defeats. Fourth, the ultimate defeat of Israel would require a revitalization of the Arab world, which may take decades or even longer to accomplish and which will necessitate a cultural, political, and economic revolution. Finally, the recovery of the Golan Heights, although essential, is not sufficient and the ultimate objective must be to recapture all Arab lands lost to Israel.

Since 1973, Syrian military doctrine has focused on the notion of "strategic parity."[6] The basic conception of this doctrine is that to defeat Israel, Syria will have to achieve a strategic balance with it. In its broadest definition, this refers to much more than

---

[6] A useful review of Syrian strategic thinking is provided by a "Senior Intelligence Analyst" in "Syria: The Strategic Threat," *IDF Journal*, Vol. III, No. 1 (Fall 1985), pp. 73-76. For discussions of the Syrian concept of "strategic parity," see three valuable essays contained in Robert Satloff, ed., *Strategy and Defense in the Eastern Mediterranean: An American Israeli Dialogue* (Washington, D.C.: The Washington Institute for Near East Policy, 1987): Itamar Rabinovich, "Political Aspects of Syrian Strategy," pp. 60-68, Amos Gilboa, "Syria's Strategic Concept," pp. 69-74, and Ze'ev Schiff, "In the Wake of Lebanon: Israel-Syria Military Balance," pp. 75-78.

just military parity, as noted by Asad:

> When we raised the slogan of strategic bal-
> ance several years ago, we realized that this
> does not only mean balancing a tank with a
> tank and a gun with a gun, but also balancing
> all aspects of life – the political, manpower, so-
> cial, cultural, economic, and military aspects.
> Neglecting any of these elements will in-
> evitably create a weakness in the body of this
> balance of which we are speaking. We also re-
> alized that this matter cannot be achieved
> overnight, but will require the appropriate
> time and effort.[7]

During the 1970s, the main effort was concentrated on the building of alliances with other Arab states on the Eastern Front – Jordan, Iraq, Saudi Arabia, and Kuwait. However, since the late 1970s, which saw the Camp David agreements remove Egypt from the list of Israel's enemies and a worsening of relations with Iraq and Jordan, Syrian defense doctrine has placed the main emphasis on efforts to strengthen its own military capabilities.

The Syrians recognized that they would have to expand and modernize their military forces if they were going to assume leadership of the anti-Israel coalition. At the same time, the removal of Egypt and Iraq from active participation in the Arab-Israeli conflict made the Syrians acutely aware of their own military vulnerability. They feared that Israel would take advantage of this weakness to launch an attack. For this reason, the initial goal of the Syrian military build-up was to create a deterrent and simultaneously

---

[7] *Damascus Domestic Service in Arabic,* March 8, 1986, as translated in FBIS, *Daily Report: Middle East and Africa,* March 10,
1986, pp. H1-H2.

to develop the capability of launching an offensive against Israel. Although Syria believed that it had to confront Israel whenever and wherever possible, it did not expect that it would have to carry out a full-scale attack on its own.[8]

The Syrians appear to have recognized that the time frames for these two objectives might not be the same. Deterrence requires that the Syrians be able to extract such a high cost that Israel would be reluctant to launch an attack. On the other hand, their doctrine mandated creation of an offensive capability with a mix of military forces able to:

- achieve strategic surprise;

- deliver a shattering, coordinated first strike on a wide array of primary Israeli military targets, especially air bases, equipment prepositioning sites, and reserve mobilization centers;

- rapidly penetrate relatively thin Israeli defenses to a pre-determined limited line of advance;

- hold this ground for enough time to create a new geostrategic reality, through diplomatic action, superpower restraint on Israel, or the active entry into combat of military forces.

Part of the Syrian objective may be to create deterrent forces that work even after a limited Syrian attack, in order to control Israeli responses. This would ensure that Israel does not feel able to expand the scope of a less-than-all-out war and thus cannot attack strategic

---

[8] Gilboa, "Syria's Strategic Concept," p. 70, notes that "Syria is able to maintain a constant state of belligerency without actually going to war, because it is an ideological state that has no sense of urgency about fulfilling its long-term goals."

targets in the rear. The forces to accomplish these objectives include:

- an air defense system to nullify Israel's air superiority over the battlefield and to protect Syrian strategic targets, based on a range of surface-to-air missile systems, optically-guided anti-aircraft weapons, modern interceptors, advanced command and control systems, a modern radar system capable of detecting aircraft at low altitudes and in all weather, and secure communications;

- a deep strike capability for use against Israeli air bases and other strategic targets to maximize the Syrian military advantage in the crucial phase between the outbreak of hostilities and the completion of Israeli call-up procedures, relying on mobile surface-to-surface missiles, advanced air-to-surface missiles, long-range artillery (including rocket artillery), and heliborne and sea-landed commando units;

- mobile ground forces, including armored units with modern tanks, mechanized infantry, commandos, specialized engineers, new and improved logistic capabilities, new and anti-tank units, protected by effective local air defenses and provided with night-fighting capabilities, enhanced munitions, and improved, secure communications;

- a navy able to threaten both strategic targets in Israel's coastal areas and lines of communication, using surface ships capable of carrying over-the-horizon antiship missiles and effective electronic defenses and submarines;

- strategic weapons, such as Scud surface-to-surface missiles armed with chemical warheads, both as a potential offensive weapon and to deter Israeli actions that might extend the limits of a conflict beyond boundaries established by Syria.

These forces would be supported by real-time intelligence and command and control systems. The Syrians will have plenty of time, during the planning stages for war, to acquire precise targeting information on a wide variety of Israeli targets that cannot be hidden. Israel is a small country, in close proximity to Syria, and thus extremely prone to intelligence penetration. A Syrian reconnaissance aircraft can "see" all of Israel from under 25,000 feet, and this without leaving Syrian airspace. The Syrians also have extremely good electronic intercept capabilities and are reported to receive satellite and radio intercept intelligence from the Soviets on a permanent basis. In consequence, it can be assumed that Syria knows the precise location of Israeli airfields, command posts, radar positions, equipment storage sites, and industrial facilities.

Syrian War Options

Syria's war options are limited by internationally guaranteed agreements with Israel that restrict force deployments.[9] Just as these agreements affect the

---

[9] The Disengagement Agreement, signed on May 31, 1974 and supervised by the United Nations force, separates the two countries with a no-man's zone and an area of limited forces. In the area within 10 kilometers of each side of the border each country can station only 2 brigades with 6000 men, 75 tanks, and 36 artillery pieces (122mm or equivalent) in the zone. In a second zone, incorporating the area that is 10 to 20 kilometers from the border, total forces are limited to 450 tanks and 162 artillery pieces (with a range of no more than 20 kilometers). No surface-to-air missiles are allowed within 25 kilometers of the border. See IDF Spokesman, *The Golan Heights,* December 15, 1981, pp. 19-23.

manner in which Syria may initiate a war, so geographic limits will affect the manner in which they fight a war. The topography of the Golan Heights (and Lebanon, for that matter) confines the Syrians to well-defined routes of advance. The Golan Heights is a relatively small area. The border between Israel and Syria is only some 80 kilometers long, not all of it suitable for mobile ground warfare, and the entire area occupied by Israel since 1967 amounts to only about 1,200 square kilometers.

As will be discussed in greater detail below, the Syrian armed forces still have some very real weaknesses, which have not disappeared despite a massive military build-up that involved the acquisition of weapons worth billions of dollars. Nevertheless, these weaknesses should not obscure their considerable strengths. Notwithstanding the advantages enjoyed by Israel, the Syrian army in the 1990s will possess the means to threaten virtually every strategic target in Israel: airfields, prepositioning sites, strategic crossroads, ports, oil refining facilities, storage depots, communications sites, and transportation depots. The combined destructive power of the Syrian armed forces, even if used with considerable inefficiency, will be enough to extract heavy casualties in even a limited confrontation, and will be capable of inflicting a potentially devastating blow to Israel, militarily, economically, and in terms of national morale.

All the elements for a sudden transition from uneasy truce to war are there. Moreover, time has become real-time with early warning indicators being severely curtailed by a combination of advanced secure communications, electronic deception, camouflage techniques and a host of other technologies. All have combined to make surprise, always a danger, an even greater one. Despite its shortcomings, the Syrian military will be capable of conducting a sophisticated conflict against Israel within the context of limited national strategic objectives. Because there is no parity of deterrence between Israel and Syria, with relative cost being to Syria's advantage, these elements increase Syria's incentive for conflict. Because a Syrian first-strike has such potentially serious consequences for Israel, the probability of preemption increases. This is yet another factor that could lead to ultimate escalation and destabilization of the arena and set the stage for a war that, although possibly confined to one major front, may be more devastating than anything the Middle East has known.

So long as Syria remains isolated it is possible to conceive of a war erupting in four different ways. First, the Syrians could launch an all-out war, to include attacks against targets in Israel's rear areas. Second, they could launch a limited attack, intended only to recover territory in the Golan Heights. Third, they could start a war of attrition, similar in scope to those of 1968-1970 and 1973-1974. Finally, a war could break out accidentally.

Given the current balance of military power between the two countries, which Syria recognizes remains favorable to Israel, the primary objective of any premeditated attack would be political and diplomatic and not military. In such a conception, war could be justified if the non-military benefits are greater than the military and non-military costs. The Syrians would attempt to garner active support from other Arab countries, forcing those countries not involved in the struggle against Israel to commit themselves or risk possible domestic and international political opposition. And, even if the Syrians were unable to capture and retain any territory on the Golan Heights, the results would be positive if it were possible to inflict heavy casualties and if the economic, political, psychological, and social repercussions in Israel were sufficiently destructive.

1) All-Out War: This would involve a massive, co-ordinated attack on Israel, aimed at the reconquest of the Golan Heights, and at inflicting maximum damage on strategic and possibly also civilian targets inside Israel. The primary objective would be to weaken Israel's long-term ability to survive by inflicting serious military, economic, social, and political damage.

Under present circumstances, this approach poses serious problems for the Syrians. With the balance of military power overwhelmingly in Israel's favor, they cannot assume that the outcome of a major war would be favorable. Nor can they count on any external support, military or political, to prevent Israel from taking advantage of its superiority, since the Soviet Union has made known its opposition to military adventures and no other Arab state is at present willing to commit itself to the war option. Moreover, a massive attack would involve a significant gamble. The Israeli forces are sufficiently strong to inflict a decisive military defeat on Syria. No matter what was accomplished, the results would be catastrophic if the ultimate outcome was a weak Syria unable to continue the struggle or to lead the anti-Israel effort. A Syrian defeat also could prejudice the rest of the Arab world against the military option for a long time.[10] Thus, there are good reasons for doubting that the Syrians would adopt this option until significant changes take place in the general

---

[10] Rabinovich, "Political Aspects of Syrian Strategy," p. 67, argues that Asad "has to take into account the possibility that his legacy may be completely demolished by an ill-calculated war with Israel."

strategic environment.

2) *Limited War:* This would be restricted to the Golan Heights. The primary military objective would be to capture and retain at least some Israeli-occupied territory, to demonstrate the continued viability of the military option. It is likely that Syria would count on an internationally-imposed cease-fire to prevent a decisive Israeli counter-strike. Nevertheless, this option also poses problems for the Syrians. Israel made it known that a limited war could easily be transformed into a general war under conditions favorable to Israel. There also could be a high political price, since the Syrians would have to abandon the United Nations-sponsored Israel-Syria disengagement accord, which is backed by the Soviet Union. Currently, the Syrians can count on Soviet support if Israel attacks Syrian territory, but this guarantee might be jeopardized if Syria initiates hostilities.

3) *War of Attrition:* The aim would be to cause Israeli casualties, but with limits on the scope, intensity, and area of the fighting. This would demonstrate the continued validity of the war option, inflict maximum costs on Israel (economic, social, political), and at the same time minimize Syrian risks. The advantages to Syria are evident, since it would pursue the war option without endangering its long-term fighting capabilities. The dangers are similar to those of the limited war option discussed above.

4) *Accidental War:* In some ways the most dangerous scenario. This could erupt as a result of friction between the two countries in Lebanon, where the Syrians have important interests. It is possible that Syria could take steps in Lebanon that would provoke

a stronger-than-anticipated Israeli response. But the Syrians have shown considerable agility in avoiding such conflicts.[11] This was demonstrated in late 1985 and early 1986, during the crisis that developed when the Israelis responded strongly to the movement of Syrian surface-to-air missiles to positions on the Syrian border with Lebanon to provide air defense for the Bekaa. Despite Israel's destruction of two Syrian MiG-23s inside Syrian territory, the leadership in Damascus never let matters get out of control.

Whether a future regime would be as adept as the existing one is not certain. A leadership that is less stable and more willing to allow domestic political factors to set diplomatic and military responses, may not be able or willing to exert the kind of control that Hafiz al-Asad has shown since he took power. This scenario is probably more dangerous for Syria than for Israel. Neither side would have the advantage of surprise, and the type of situation in which a conflict of this type would break out would tend to be one in which the Syrians are less able to control political and diplomatic circumstances needed to turn defeat into victory.

The belief that the chances of war between Israel and Syria in the immediate future are extremely low is shared by strategic planners in Israel and intelligence analysts in the United States. It is considered unlikely that the Syrians will intentionally initiate a war until they are able to achieve a comprehensive "strategic balance" with Israel. The current political climate makes it unlikely that there

---

[11] Gilboa, "Syria's Strategic Concept," p. 72, suggests that "despite Syria's belief in the use of force, actual Syrian behavior has proven to be very pragmatic and cautious."

will be general Arab participation in a war in pursuit of Syrian national goals, the only alternative to Syria achieving parity on its own.

The Defeat in Lebanon

During the years that immediately followed Egyptian President Anwar Sadat's 1977 trip to Jerusalem, the Syrian military acquired armaments worth more than $8 billion, according to official U.S. government estimates (See table, page 43).[12] As a result, by the time of the 1982 Lebanon War the Syrians had an impressive arsenal. Its military forces were considerably larger than in 1973, and the quality of the armaments was far superior.

The 1982 War, however, demonstrated with vivid clarity the disparity between force strength on paper and real battle capability. The equipment that Syria had acquired was shown to be fallible, and the presumed answers to Israeli air superiority, largely mythical.[13] Despite its impressive size, the Syrian war machine was still extremely vulnerable. Front-line Soviet aircraft and missiles were inferior to the Western equipment possessed by Israel; Soviet air doctrine, dependent on ground-to-air communications, fallible; Soviet radar, electronics, and communications equipment, obsolescent. Soviet sys-

---

[12] Arms Control and Disarmament Agency, *World Military Expenditures and Arms Transfers 1986* (Washington, D.C.: Government Printing Office, 1987), p. 137.

[13] Richard Gabriel, *Operation Peace for Galilee* (New York: Hill and Wang, 1984), p. 121, reports that Syria lost 90 aircraft, 6 Gazelle antitank helicopters, and 19 surface-to-air missile batteries.

tems that had seemed highly effective in 1973 were easily defeated in 1982. In 1973 Israel lost 25 percent of its air force to surface-to-air missiles, but in June 1982 the Syrians were unable to shoot down a single Israeli aircraft.

Critical was the fact that Israel enjoyed superiority not only in the air, but of the airwaves as well. The Soviet-Syrian perspective is reflected in the observations of one Soviet analyst on the Israeli attacks on the Syrians.

> In the course of preparing for and conducting the 1982 war, the Israeli Air Force command possessed reliable information on the electronic equipment and electronic systems for controlling Syrian air defenses and air force. This made it possible for the aggressor with minimal losses in a short period of time to win supremacy in the skies of Lebanon.[14]

American and Soviet studies of the 1982 fighting strongly suggest that Israel's successes cannot be attributed solely to the superior quality of its pilots and fighter aircraft. While one cannot belittle the role of the Israeli pilot, his mission – air-to-ground or air-to-air – was virtually assured of success before he took off. Accurate intelligence information made it possible for Israeli commanders to anticipate Syrian actions. Indeed, according to a Soviet expert, the Israelis had so much information about Syrian air operations that "Israeli fighters scrambled simultaneously with (or even 1 or 2 minutes before) the take-off of the Syrian aircraft" that they were to

---

[14] S.V. Seroshtan, "Local Wars," *Voyenno-Istoricheskiy Zurnal*, No. 3, 1986, as translated by U.S. Joint Publication Research Service, "Electronic Combat in Local Wars in Near East," UMA-86-047, pp. 70-71.

intercept. With RF-4E reconnaissance aircraft and drones, airborne electronic intercept aircraft (especially E-2Cs and modified Boeing 707s), and ground-based electronic intelligence systems, Israeli commanders had at their disposal a comprehensive electronic order of battle. This made it possible for them to dissect the Syrian air defenses with almost surgical precision. Syrian communications were jammed. Surface-to-air missile batteries were made inoperative. Decoys prevented Syrian air defenses from locating Israeli aircraft. Air defense systems were destroyed by a combination of air- and ground-launched ordnance, much of it operated from beyond Syrian range. All this was made possible by Israel's highly effective C^3 system.[15]

The integrated Israeli assault on the Syrian air defense system exposed substantial, unexpected vulnerabilities in critical areas. Moreover, it showed that Israel had the ability to employ unexpected means, largely because of the operational and technological ingenuity of Israeli military planners and technical experts.

Vulnerable, however, did not mean vanquished. From Asad's perspective Syria was defeated only technologically, and the Soviet Union was to blame. The Syrian military, for its part, having been taken almost completely by surprise, intentionally limited the conflict by sending only a few reinforcements to Lebanon, and did not open up a second front on the Golan Heights. Thus, the Syrians were fighting un-

---

[15] Seroshtan, "Local Wars," pp. 69-75, provides a comprehensive analysis of this aspect of the 1982 war. See also W. Seth Carus, "Military Lessons of the 1982 Israel-Syria Conflict," pp. 261-270, in Robert Harkavy and Stephanie Neuman, eds., *The Lessons of Recent Wars in the Third World* (Lexington, Mass.: Lexington Books, 1985).

der particularly unfavorable circumstances.

The Syrians had reason to be pleased with the performance of their ground forces which often fought very competently, with the commando units doing extremely well. Many formations stood their ground in the face of overwhelming odds, and their front did not collapse despite Israeli forces superior in quality and quantity. Finally, many Syrian officers demonstrated tactical ability and courage under adverse conditions.

The Soviet-Syrian Response

Although some of its forces performed well, the collapse of its air defenses and the decisive defeat of the Syrian Air Force made it clear that Syria had to revise its responses to the Israeli challenge. Despite some reluctance, the Soviets had an incentive to assist the Syrian effort, for reasons that went beyond the immediate goal of restoring Syria's military credibility. Many of the Syrian systems destroyed by Israel in the Bekaa were identical to those used by the Soviet Union's East European allies, and those countries felt the reverberations of Israel's success as keenly as Damascus.

The joint Syrian-Soviet response manifested itself in three main ways.

- First, the Soviet Union quickly replaced equipment lost by the Syrians, including aircraft, missile batteries, and tanks.

- Second, new systems were supplied to correct weaknesses revealed during the 1982 fighting. Especially important were the expansion and modernization of Syrian air defenses and C^3I systems.

- Third, new systems were introduced into the

Syrian military in areas where the Soviets and Syrians perceived possible Israeli vulnerabilities.

By the winter of 1982 the modernization program was well underway.

An essential component of the build-up was a restructuring of the air defenses. These had been assigned a central role in Syria's defense doctrine since after the 1967 war, but in 1982 it was evident that they were unable to prevent Israeli aircraft from freely operating over Syrian ground forces and that the anti-aircraft systems were highly vulnerable to Israeli attack. The revitalization was both quantitative and qualitative. The number of medium-range surface-to-air missile batteries, was increased dramatically from 100 in 1982 to 180 in 1987. It is believed that the number of short-range SA-9 launchers also grew, but no conclusive evidence is available.

More significant was the accompanying qualitative enhancement. Long-range coverage that extended well into Israeli territory was provided by three new SA-5 batteries. These missiles were acquired from the Soviet Union in 1983 to counter Israeli airborne-intelligence systems, such as the Boeing 707 electronic warfare and the E-2C airborne-early warning aircraft. Other new types of missiles also were acquired, including the vehicle-mounted SA-13 and possibly the hand-held SA-14 (an equivalent to the American Stinger). Syria also may have received a small number of mobile SA-11 missile launchers in the past few years as well.[16]

---

[16] Aharon Levran and Zeev Eytan, *The Middle East Military Balance 1986* (Boulder, Colorado: Westview Press, 1987), provides details of the Syrian air defenses. "The SA-11 Gadfly

A primary characteristic of the new air defense system is its enhanced mobility. Most of the new missile batteries are vehicle-mounted: it is estimated that about 100 of the batteries are equipped with mobile SA-6, SA-8, or SA-11 missile launchers. The bulk of the batteries have SA-8s, which are mobile (they can be quickly moved from position to position); easy to conceal (it is not easy to distinguish SA-8 launchers from other trucks); and autonomous (each launcher can operate in isolation, even if communications are disrupted). Similarly, low-altitude air defenses now count on additional numbers of SA-9 and SA-13 vehicle-mounted launchers, and the total inventory of self-propelled anti-aircraft guns now may exceed 550 (300 23mm ZSU-23-4 radar-guided guns and 250 57mm ZSU-57-2 optically-guided guns).[17]

The 300 ZSU-23-4 guns is far more than normally would be expected for an army the size of Syria's. By comparison, it was estimated in 1985 that the East German army had only 96 ZSU-23-4s, that Hungary had 75, and Poland 130.[18] The Soviet Union assigns only 16 ZSU-23-4s to a division, so that an army the size of Syria's, with only 8 armored and mechanized divisions, would normally have 128 such vehicles. In fact, it has at least two-and-a-half times more than that. Indeed, the Syrians have a significant

---

missile system," *Jane's Defence Weekly*, July 5, 1986, p. 3103, indicates that since 1983 it has been reported that Syria has the SA-11.

[17] The Jordanians stated in 1983 that the Syrians had 700 air defense guns, including 300 ZSU-23-4s and 250 self-propelled ZSU-57-2s. See "Israelis Penetrate Jordanian Airspace," *Aviation Week & Space Technology*, June 27, 1983, pp. 56.

[18] International Institute for Strategic Studies, *Military Balance 1985-1986* (London: International Institute for Strategic Studies, 1985), pp. 32-35.

proportion of all the self-propelled artillery manufactured for export by the Soviet Union. According to one U.S. report, the Soviet Union built 1,600 self-propelled anti-aircraft guns for export between 1972 and 1983. It appears that more than 20% of them went to Syria.[19]

The Soviet Union also provided enhanced information-gathering and command and control capabilities. New radars were supplied, including the vehicle-mounted Long Track surveillance systems never before supplied to a Middle Eastern country.[20] The Syrians also have taken steps to improve their command and control capabilities and to make their air defense communications less vulnerable to Israeli interference. The Soviet Union has provided Syria with a new generation of command and control systems that Israel should find more difficult to incapacitate than the equipment used in 1982. At the same time, however, the air defense system is less dependent on centralized command and control than the system employed in 1982. The emphasis has been placed on acquiring weapons that can operate autonomously if necessary: the SA-8, SA-9, SA-11, SA-13, and ZSU-23-4 are all self-contained systems with the detection and fire-control electronics and the weapon mounted on a single vehicle. Thus, even if the new command and control system is completely incapacitated the Syrians would retain a potent air defense capability.

The Syrians also took steps to enhance their ground forces. The Syrian army grew from six divi-

---

[19] *Aerospace Daily,* August 31, 1984, p. 349, reprint of a U.S. Defense Intelligence Agency table that originally appeared in *Congressional Record,* August 10, 1984.

[20] *Aerospace Daily,* October 27, 1982, p. 305.

sions to nine, including additional armored divisions and a special forces division. Regular army manpower grew from 240,000 in 1982 to about 396,000 in 1986. The quality of equipment improved, with the addition of 600 new T-72 tanks and the acquisition of additional self-propelled artillery pieces. Existing tanks were improved through the addition of laser rangefinders, night vision devices, reactive armor, secure communications systems, fire control computers, and enhanced ammunition. Stress was placed on the acquisition of attack helicopters. At the same time, the Soviets provided equipment and training to greatly enhance Syrian command and control, electronic warfare, and logistic capabilities, including remotely piloted vehicles of various types.[21]

Steps were also taken to enhance Syria's "deep strike" capabilities. The number of surface-to-surface missile launchers increased from 35 to 53, including acquisition of 12 SS-21 launchers. These new missiles are significantly more accurate than the existing Frog and Scud missiles.[22] The commando units, which fought so well in Lebanon, were expanded in size, and the total number of commando groups grew from nine to 35. Most of them have been organized into a single division, but there are still seven independent groups. The Syrian air force has been able to enhance its attack capabilities by acquiring air-to-surface missiles and other special-

---

[21] Based on various editions of the *Middle East Military Balance*.

[22] A detailed study of Syrian surface-to-surface missile forces is Joseph S. Bermudez, Jr., "The Syrian Missile Threat," *Marine Corps Gazette,* January 1985, pp. 54-62.

ized ordnance.[23]

The Slow-Down of Syrian Military Expansion

Starting in 1985 there were indications that the Syrian build-up had run into difficulties. By 1986 it was clear that the Syrians had bitten off more than they could chew and that the modernization program was grinding to a halt. Large scale maneuvers scheduled for the spring and summer of 1985 and 1986 were cancelled and the expenditure of live ammunition in training was curtailed. Training never progressed as far as planned, and many divisions did not complete their training programs. Soldiers were demobilized, some equipment was mothballed, and some combat units were deactivated. Additional brigades that were planned for incorporation into existing divisions were not created. Difficulties were encountered in absorbing new command and control technologies. Systems in the pipeline were not delivered as planned, and MiG-29 fighters originally scheduled for delivery in late 1986 remained undelivered through the summer of 1987.[24]

The build-up came to a halt for many reasons, but the most important single factor was probably Syria's economic distress. The economy declined in size during the 1980s: according to one estimate, Syria's

-----

[23] Figures derived from various editions of the *Middle East Military Balance*.

[24] Arms Control and Disarmament Agency, *World Military Expenditures and Arms Transfers 1986*, p. 137, indicates that arms imports declined from $1.5 billion in 1984 to only $925 million in 1985.

gross domestic product was 3% smaller in real terms in 1986 than it had been in 1981. In 1986 alone the economy probably declined more than 2%.[25] The economic difficulties were largely a result of structural weaknesses caused by inept management of the economy by the government, reflected in the massive investments devoted to a poorly conceived industrialization effort. The structural problems were exacerbated by excessive levels of military spending, a reduction in revenues resulting from the drop in oil prices, and a decline in economic aid from Iran and Arab countries.[26]

Syria was hard-pressed to pay for arms imports, due to a lack of foreign exchange, and there was even a shortage of cash needed to sustain domestic defense spending. According to Ze'ev Schiff, the Syrian military budget for fiscal year 1987-1988 dropped by 15% in real terms compared with the previous year, a reduction of about $500 million.[27]

By early 1988, however, the Syrian military again showed signs of renewed activity. After a long period of dormancy, training schedules were accelerated and more large-scale maneuvers held.

---

[25] "Syria: grim times now, better prospects ahead," *Middle East Economic Digest*, April 11, 1987, pp. 36-37.

[26] For a detailed discussion, see Eliyahu Kanovsky, "What's Behind Syria's Current Economic Problems," pp. 280-347, in *Middle East Contemporary Survey*, Volume VIII: 1983-1984 (Tel Aviv: The Dayan Center for Middle East and African Studies, The Shiloah Institute, Tel Aviv University, 1986).

[27] Ze'ev Schiff, presentation at a Washington Institute for Near East Policy Symposium on "From Deterrence to Peace: The Spectrum of Arab-Israeli Relations in the 1980s," April 8, 1987.

There also were impressive qualitative improvements made in Syria's armored forces, specifically in terms of all-weather, day-night capabilities, and in the complete mobilization of its artillery forces. There were notable improvements in the air force, with the delivery of the MiG-29 and it appears that Su-24 strike fighters will be supplied by the end of 1989. The navy was bolstered by new submarines, frigates, and missiles.[28]

Notwithstanding these developments, however, Syria remains a country with severe economic and diplomatic problems, and is still strategically isolated. These difficulties continue to constrain Syria's military activities, and prevent President Asad from creating military forces as potent as those desired.

Changing Soviet Attitudes

Also problematic for the Syrians were shifting Soviet attitudes towards Syria and the Middle East, especially evident during Asad's April 1987 trip to Moscow. Soviet leader Mikhail Gorbachev noted that "the stake on military power in settling the conflict has become completely discredited," and Soviet commentaries added that "the use of force and fresh outbreaks of war would be fraught with the most serious consequences."[29] This stands in sharp con-

---

[28] Interview on *Jerusalem Television Service* (Arabic), August 30, 1988, as translated in FBIS, *Daily Report: Near East and South Asia,* August 31, 1988, p. 23.

[29] Moscow *Pravda* in Russian, April 25, 1987, pp. 1-2, second edition, as translated in FBIS, *Daily Report: USSR International,* April 28, 1987, pp. H2, H7.

trast to earlier Syrian arguments in connection with
the Golan Heights that "what has been taken by
force can be restored only by force."[30] Thus, the Soviets indicated their opposition to a military strategy
that involved a Syrian initiation of armed hostilities.
At the same time, Soviet disagreements with Syria
over Lebanon and the PLO remained acute. Also
inhibiting the relationship was Soviet willingness to
take steps to improve relations with Egypt and Israel,
to end the Iran-Iraq war, and to limit points of
confrontation with the West in the context of Gorbachev's grand strategy.[31] Soviet policy toward Syria
was further tempered by a desire not to antagonize
Iraq by supplying Syria, Iran's major Arab supporter
in the Gulf War, with advanced weapons.

The change in Soviet attitudes was reflected in
the decision during the summer of 1987 not to supply
Syria with SS-23 surface-to-surface missiles.[32] The
SS-23 is accurate to a range of 500 kilometers,
covering all of Israel, in contrast to the two missile

---

[30] Syrian Defense Minister Mustafa Talas, in *Al-Majallah*
(London), 11-17 December 1985, p. 11, in Arabic, as
translated in FBIS, *Daily Report: Middle East and Africa,*
December 12, 1985, p. H1.

[31] See Elaine Sciolino, "Syria Has Tried to Keep Its Ties to the
Russians Elastic," *New York Times,* January 26, 1986.

[32] Reports of Syrian interest in obtaining SS-23 surface-to-surface missiles surfaced in the spring of 1986. By the summer of
1987 it was evident that the Soviets had decided to reject the
Syrian request. See Re'ueven Pedatzur, "Military Involvement
As a Political Tool," *Ha'aretz,* July 28, 1987, p. 13, in Hebrew
as translated in FBIS, *Daily Report: Middle East and Africa,* July
29, 1987, pp. L4-L5, and Jim Hoagland and Patrick Tyler,
"Reduced Soviet Arms Flow Weakens Syrian Military,"
Washington Post, September 25, 1987, p. A1.

systems already supplied. The 100-kilometer range of the highly accurate SS-21 limits it to targets only in northern Israel. And although the Scud missiles have sufficient range to hit southern Israel they are extremely inaccurate. For these reasons, a Soviet decision to supply Syria with SS-23 missiles had long been feared by Israel. Similarly, when the Soviet Union finally agreed to supply MiG-29 fighters, originally scheduled for delivery in late 1986 and early 1987, they were not delivered until late 1987 and the versions provided lacked the sophisticated electronics of the standard Soviet model.[33] There were also indications that the Syrians were not pleased with the quality of the SA-5 missiles and other systems that had been supplied to them by the Soviets.[34]

The cold war in relations between Syria and the Soviet Union began to ease in early 1987. It appears that in the wake of the Asad visit to Moscow in the spring of 1987, the Soviets agreed to ship the long-delayed MiG-29s, and in early 1988 a substantial arms agreement was negotiated. This new agreement included additional MiG-29 fighters, T-72

---

[33] According to Israeli Defense Minister Yitzhak Rabin, as cited by *Jerusalem Domestic Service* in Hebrew, September 30, 1987, as translated in FBIS, *Daily Report: Near East and South Asia,* September 30, 1987, p. 22.

[34] By early 1985 it appears that the Syrians were demanding a more sophisticated version of the missile than the type originally supplied in 1982/1983. See Kuwait *Kuna* in English, February 4, 1986, as given in FBIS, *Daily Report: USSR International Affairs,* February 11, 1986, p. H1. The ineffectiveness of the SA-5s used by Libya in April 1986 against the U.S. Navy cannot have increased Syrian confidence in their SA-5s.

tanks, SS-21 missiles, and the Su-24 strike fighter. The Su-24 is equivalent in capabilities to the American F-111 bomber. It had never been exported by the Soviets. The implications of this sale are not yet clear, but it is evident that the Soviets remain willing to supply Syria with high quality armaments.

By late 1986 it was clear to the Syrians that their military options were severely limited by circumstances over which they had little control. Although there was no evidence of an inclination to abandon the long-term struggle, Syria could no longer expect to make significant increases in its military power. The growth of the Syrian military in the late 1980s would have to be far more modest than originally anticipated. For example, rather than buying new, advanced tanks, it appears that the Syrians have had to be content with improvements in their old T-55 and T-62 tanks.

It is evident that the Syrians have fallen far short of their aim of reaching military equality with Israel. Nevertheless, the military force that they have created is impressive in many respects. Because of its ability to inflict heavy casualties on Israel, it provides the Syrians with a potent deterrent to Israeli action. Moreover, they have managed to lay the foundations for a modern, efficient, integrated army that could, if used correctly, change the geopolitical status quo of the Middle East.

New Technologies and Syrian Military Power

The question remains to what degree the Syrians will be able to adapt to an era of technological innovation. New technologies require new skills and more training. The greater the integration of forces, the greater the need for advanced management skills. The gap between theoretical and real strength, as demonstrated by the Lebanon War, is not an esoteric calculation for the Syrians. They operate under an inherent double disadvantage in their quest for strategic parity with Israel, since both the systems and the manpower at their disposal are inferior to those possessed by Israel and will remain so.

Moreover, the Israelis have demonstrated an ability to isolate and attack Syrian weak points, rather than confront Syria frontally, complicating the task of Syrian military planners. Ultimately, military capabilities cannot be measured by examining the performance of military equipment. More important is how that equipment will be utilized in unpredictable situations dictated by the enemy and to what degree a force will be able to maintain its offensive momentum in the face of unexpected enemy actions. Thus, it is not enough for the Syrians to be reactive, eliminating their own weaknesses and searching for past Israeli weaknesses. They must also be able to act in creative ways under the stress of combat.

The emergence of new technologies is especially problematic for the Syrians. It is not certain that the Soviet Union will be able to supply Syria with the kinds of equipment that they will need to compete in the new environment. Even if the Soviets are able to develop the equipment for their own use, it is not self-evident that it would automatically be supplied to Syria.

An even more important calculation revolves around the impact that the new systems will have on existing force structures. They could reduce the value of military forces central to Syrian defense doctrine. As a result, the Syrians may find that the battlefield effectiveness of their forces could deteriorate in the coming years, and that the deterrent capabilities of their forces may be significantly reduced.

Syrian air defenses will not be able to effectively protect rear areas or combat units from attack. The availability of a new generation of deep-attack weapons and of effective alternatives to close air support for ground forces means that the value of Syrian air defenses will decrease. The Syrians have made heavy investments in air defenses to counter Israel's air strength, and the continued danger from this source will prevent them from reducing these defenses in the foreseeable future. Yet, the air defenses will not provide protection against the new generation of deep-attack weapons, long-range, air-launched or ground-launched munitions. Israel's capability in this area will thus reduce the impact of Syria's extensive air defense network.

Moreover the value of massed tank attacks will be reduced by the new generation of antitank weapons, again degrading a key Syrian military capability. The ability of long-range sensors to track mass tank movements, coupled with the availability of weapons to attack such formations, makes the Syrian armored columns vulnerable even far from the front. Although it may be possible to adopt tactics that minimize exposure to this threat, this may lead to reduced mobility and greater dispersion and a resulting reduction in offensive capabilities.

The Syrian military will gain some advantages from the new technologies, even in the short-term. Syrian intelligence-gathering capabilities are growing, as exemplified by the acquisition of remotely-piloted vehicles. Rear area attack capabilities are also improving due to the availability of accurate surface-to-air and air-to-surface missiles, and improved helicopters.

The final balance for the Syrians of benefits and losses accruing from the new technologies will not be fully known for some time. But it is clear that they have reason to view the future battlefield with some concern. They have not demonstrated an ability to compete in the new environment, and there are reasons to believe that many of the important factors, especially the vital role of high-quality manpower, are areas of traditional Israeli advantage. (This subject will be raised again in chapter 7: The Human Context of the New Technologies, p. 133).

(TABLE 1)
SYRIAN ARMS IMPORTS
1975-1985

Year	Arms Imports ($ millions)	Total Arms Imports ($ millions)
1975	380	380
1976	625	1,005
1977	650	1,655
1978	900	2,555
1979	2,100	4,655
1980	2,700	7,355
1981	2,200	9,555
1982	2,300	11,855
1983	2,000	13,855
1984	1,500	15,355
1985	925	16,280
Total	16,280	

Source: Arms Control and Disarmament Agency, *World Military Expenditures and Arms Transfers 1986* (Washington, D.C.: Government Printing Office, 1987), p. 137.

(TABLE 2)
SYRIAN ORDER OF BATTLE
1973-1987

	1973	1982	1987
Divisions			
Armored	2	3	5
Mechanized	3	3	4
Commando	0	0	1
Total Divisions	5	6	10
Army Equipment			
Battle tanks	2,100	3,600	4,100
Personnel carriers	1,500	2,700	3,500
Guns and mortars	1,330	2,300	2,300
Antitank missile launchers	360	2,000	2,000
Tactical ballistic missile launchers	12	35	53
Combat Aircraft			
Interceptors	200	224	360
Strike and multi-role	110	225	290
Attack helicopters	0	?	90
Air Defenses			
Long-range missile batteries	34	107	180
Anti-aircraft guns	?	1,000	1,000

Source: Compilation from Aharon Levran and Zeev Eytan, *The Middle East Military Balance 1986* (Boulder, Colorado: Westview Press, 1987), various editions of *The Military Balance* published annually by the London-based International Instititute for Strategic Studies, and from a wide variety of other published sources.

(TABLE 3)
SYRIAN ARMS ACQUISITIONS:
Ground, Air, Naval
1982-1986

Army Equipment
> T-62/T-72 battle tanks
> BMP infantry fighting vehicles
> SAU-122 self-propelled 122mm howitzers
> SAU-152 self-propelled 155mm howitzers
> BM-21 multiple rocket launchers
> AT-4 antitank missile launchers
> SS-21 tactical ballistic missile launchers
> Cluster artillery ammunition

Combat Aircraft/Helicopters/Aircraft Ordnance
> MiG-29 fighters
> MiG-25 interceptors
> MiG-27 fighter-bombers
> MiG-23 fighters
> Su-22 attack aircraft
> Mi-24 Hind attack helicopters
> Mi-8 Hip electronic warfare helicopters
> Gazelle helicopters (from France)
> Laser-guided bombs
> Antiradiation missiles

Naval Systems
> 3   Romeo-class submarines
> 4   Nanuchka-class missile corvettes
> 4   Osa II missile boats
> 2   Polnocny amphibious ships
>   SSC-1 Sepal coastal defense missiles
>   SSC-3 Styx coastal defense missiles

Source: Compilation from press reports.

(TABLE 4)
SYRIAN ARMS ACQUISITIONS:
Air Defense Systems
1982-1986

SA-5 missile batteries
SA-6 missile batteries
SA-8 mobile missile launchers
SA-9 mobile missile launchers
SA-13 mobile missile launchers
SA-14 hand-held missile launchers
ZSU-23-4 self-propelled anti-aircraft guns
Long Track mobile search radars
Area search radars
Command and control systems

Source: Compilation from press reports.

3: The Israeli Dimension

Predicting Israel's future regime is far easier than trying to understand the nature of a future Syria. Notwithstanding the potential complications that could result from Israel's continued occupation of the West Bank and Gaza (or, conversely, the consequences of negotiating their status), it is almost certain that in the 1990s, as now, Israel will basically be a stable, democratic country, oriented toward the West and closely allied with the United States.

Israeli Strategic Assumptions

The interaction between complex economic, social, and military factors in Israel, coupled with the immediacy of the threat of war, the unpredictability of the arena, and the horrendous cost of potential error, present Israeli planners with a difficult set of choices. In the back of their minds looms the specter of the 1973 October War, which resulted in the loss of 2,838 dead and 8,800 wounded and economic costs of $7.1 billion.[1] They know that the destructiveness of future weapons could make the price of any future failure much higher.

They also must deal with the strategic reality that 90 percent of Israel's population, some 90 percent of its industrial infrastructure, two of its three main ports, its entire oil refining capacity, and almost all its airports, are situated on a narrow strip of land along the coast less than ten minutes flying time from Damascus.[2] Moreover, 85 percent of the Israel Defense Forces' ground units are manned by reservists, requiring 48 hours for mobilization, during which its active duty military forces have to cope with enemy threats.

Israeli military planners consistently base their assumptions on worst-case scenarios, like an end to the peace treaty with Egypt, a hostile Iraq capable of delivering significant forces to the battlefield in very short time, and Jordan and Saudi Arabia both playing a role. It is generally assumed, however, that Israel's major opponent will remain Syria and that wider Arab participation will depend largely on the duration of the conflict and the speed of superpower intervention. Nevertheless, the minimal participation of other countries is taken as a given, in the form of supplies of offensive weapons (surface-to-surface missiles, aircraft, surface vessels and submarines); support (AWACS early-warning aircraft, re-supply, second-echelon logistics, communications, intelligence); manpower (volunteers, technical and

---

[1] Hirsh Goodman, *Israel's Strategic Reality: The Impact of the Arms Race* (Washington, D.C.: The Washington Institute for Near East Policy, 1985), p. 8.

[2] Goodman, *Israel's Strategic Reality*, pp. 4-5.

irregular units); technology transfers; or financial assistance.

There appears to be a consensus among Israeli military strategists that the Air Force will remain the country's main response to external force threats, though deep-interdiction troops, attack helicopters, and precision-guided munitions will also be part of an Israeli response. Given recent reports that Israel is testing a Jericho II surface-to-surface missile with a range of at least 800 kilometers, one can assume that Israel also possesses conventional strategic responses to deter and minimize possible third force participation.[3]

The paradox, that confronts Israeli military planners is that while they recognize that Israel will retain an absolute military advantage over Syria and any likely constellation of confrontation states, many believe that Israel cannot in the final analysis win a war. The destructive capability of contemporary and future weapons, when combined with the large size of the Syrian military, the constraints on maneuver imposed by the geography of the Golan Heights, and the density of Syrian fortifications, makes it highly probable that Israel will suffer heavy casualties in a future war, even under favorable conditions. Although casualty predictions are notoriously inaccurate, it is worth noting that one analysis estimated that even if Israel achieved total strategic surprise against Syria, it would still suffer "less than 2,000 dead," and that if Syria were able to achieve strategic surprise against

---

[3] The initial story about the new missile appeared in *International Defense Review*, July 1987, p. 857. According to this report, the missile may have a range of up to 1,450 kilometers.

Israel, losses would increase to 4,500.[4] A costly war, even one that is militarily successful, is likely to be unacceptable to Israelis. This sensitivity to casualties reduces the deterrent effect of the military advantage based on technological superiority.

No matter how victorious its forces may be in the field, the costs are likely to far outweigh any gain. Every war that Israel fights undermines the country's economy, discourages immigration, encourages emigration, and kills and maims many of yet another generation of Israel's youth. The cornerstone of Israel's strategic philosophy, therefore, must be deterrence, and the main task of the IDF will not be to win a war, but to prevent one from happening.

In this context Israel has made it known that it, not the enemy, will decide on the scope of the conflict once it has broken out. In other words, even a limited military operation, by just one of the Arab countries, designed to attain a limited goal (a Syrian bid for the Golan, for example) will be treated by Israel as a total war scenario. Failing deterrence, the role of the IDF becomes to effect a speedy victory at minimum cost, while limiting the bulk of the fighting to enemy territory. This will be achieved by concentrating on the enemy's weaknesses, rather than confronting strengths, and by developing the technological means that will maximize effective response and minimize Israeli casualties.

The basic assumptions of Israeli doctrine will not change much toward the next decade from those outlined in a Rand Corporation study conducted for

---

[4] Kenneth S. Brower, "The Middle East military balance: Israel versus the rest," *International Defense Review*, July 1986, p. 912.

the Pentagon in 1981.[5] The guiding maxim will remain "a defensive strategy, executed offensively" to compensate for Israel's lack of strategic depth and its inability to retreat from the country's borders. The idea that most of the fighting must take place on enemy territory is a fundamental part of Israeli military thinking, as are the principles of offense, speed, adaptability, and minimal casualties.

Offensive operations allow the IDF to compensate for Israeli numerical inferiority by seizing the initiative, thereby dictating the place and pace of events. The IDF would concentrate forces at chosen points, attain local parity or even superiority, and seek decisive victory by swift disruption of enemy forces at critical junctures. Control of the war is seen as a means of neutralizing a large portion of enemy forces by rendering them reactive, while a fluid style of warfare fully exploits the IDF's macro-competence and simultaneously deprives the Arabs of one of their strengths: a schematic execution of prepared plans.

Economic constraints, coupled with the rising cost of new platforms, will dictate that the modernization and upgrading of the Israeli army take place at the expense of the size of the forces at all levels. The Air Force will have around one-third fewer aircraft in the 1990s than originally envisioned. The Navy will be forced to upgrade existing platforms in place of new craft acquisition. The ground forces will have fewer divisions.

---

[5] Yoav Ben-Horin and Barry Posen, *Israel's Strategic Doctrine*, R-2845-NA (Santa Monica, California: Rand Corporation, 1981).

The Casualty Factor

Israel's extreme sensitivity to casualties has been demonstrated many times and in many different contexts. Politicians and senior generals have paid heavily for the errors resulting in casualties in the past. The ouster of Golda Meir's government in 1974 was a direct consequence of the debacle of the Yom Kippur War, as were the dismissals of chief of staff David Elazar and head of military intelligence Eli Zeira. Similarly, Menachem Begin's decision to resign as Prime Minister in 1983 has been attributed to the mounting casualty rate in Lebanon.

The sinking of an Israeli destroyer, the Eilat with the loss of men, by Egyptian antiship missiles in 1967 played an important role in the decision of the Navy to rely exclusively on small boats in order to limit casualties should the enemy sink another ship. The main task facing the developers of the Merkava battle tank, sometimes at the expense of other factors, was to ensure high crew survivability. The heavy casualties suffered by the IDF armored corps during the 1973 war made armored officers acutely aware of the need to provide tank crews with as much protection as possible.[6]

This sensitivity has influenced the conduct of war and of national defense policy. Israel's decision to withdraw from most of Lebanon in June 1985 was directly linked to casualty-generated public pressure. The decision to initiate deep penetration bombing raids on Egyptian strategic and industrial targets during the 1969-1970 War of Attrition, regardless of the diplomatic consequences, was motivated in part by a concern to reduce the number of casualties that

---

6 Reuven Gal, *A Portrait of the Israeli Soldier* (Greenwood, Ct.: Greenwood Press, 1986), pp. 238-239.

Israel was suffering. Israel has consistently conducted disproportionate prisoner of war exchanges, including the 1985 exchange of 1,150 Palestinian and Shi'ite detainees for three Israeli soldiers being held by Ahmed Jibril's Popular Front for the Liberation of Palestine (PFLP).[7]

The attitude toward casualties has a major impact at the doctrinal level as well. A fundamental tenet of Israeli military training, one that is hammered home relentlessly from the first day of service to the last, is never to abandon a comrade in the field. Israeli soldiers are told that commanders will never order an operation without regard for the human cost and that no effort will be spared in bringing a wounded or captured soldier back to safety. Tremendous resources have been invested in developing speedy evacuation procedures and front-line medical facilities, reported to be among the most advanced in the world.[8]

Arab strategists consider Israel's sensitivity to casualties as one of its greatest weaknesses. Syria's President Hafiz al-Asad has often remarked that Syria's military development should be tailored with this in mind, and Syrian strategic doctrine sees a massive, quick first strike followed by a protracted war of attrition as the optimal mode of warfare,

---

[7] Gal, *A Portrait of the Israeli Soldier*, p. 238, notes that following the 1967 war Israel exchanged 561 Syrian prisoners to obtain the release of one pilot and that after the 1973 war about 8,400 Egyptians were traded for 232 Israelis and 392 Syrians for 65 Israelis.

[8] Stephen Glick, *Israeli Medical Support for the U.S. Armed Forces* (Washington, D.C.: American Israel Public Affairs Committee, 1983), pp. 8-11, provides a good summary.

mainly because of the casualty factor.[9]

It may be possible for Israel to reduce losses through technological and tactical innovation and through the careful selection of wartime objectives. Soldiers can be protected against many battlefield hazards better than in the past. The use of body armor during the 1982 Lebanon War had a significant impact on casualty levels, and it may be possible to do even more by using some of the new materials that are now being developed. The Israeli military also has done a great deal to enhance the protection offered by armored vehicles. The design of the Merkava was heavily influenced by such considerations, but even older tanks and APCs have been given better protection. Halon fire suppression systems have been fitted to most tanks and tank crews have been provided with clothes made of fire-resistant Nomex. Armor protection has been improved, most obviously through the adoption of reactive armor, which consists of explosive plates that disrupt shaped charge warheads of the type used on antitank missiles and rockets.[10] But all these steps may not be enough to reduce losses to acceptable levels.

The increased use of robotic type systems also should make it possible to cut casualties. Reliance on

---

[9] A summary of some Arab views on Israel's sensitivity to casualties is given in Steven J. Rosen, *Military Geography and the Military Balance in the Arab-Israel Conflict*, Jerusalem Papers on Peace Problems Number 21 (Jerusalem, Israel: The Leonard Davis Institute for International Relations at The Hebrew University of Jerusalem, 1977), pp. 54-55.

[10] W. Seth Carus, "Military Lessons of the 1982 Israel-Syria Conflict," pp. 271-274, in Robert Harkavy and Stephanie Neuman, eds., *The Lessons of Recent Wars in the Third World* (Lexington, Mass.: Lexington Books, 1985).

automated devices should cut down on the number of soldiers who are exposed to enemy fire. In defensive situations many soldiers may be able to fight from prepared positions, keeping the number of potentially vulnerable troops to a minimum. On the offensive, however, and especially when attacking heavily fortified positions, it will be harder to avoid casualties and losses might be very heavy. This will limit Israeli military objectives, making it difficult to launch ground attacks in the Syrian fortified belt located between Damascus and the Golan Heights.

Given the increasingly destructive nature of the weapons in the Mideast arena, coupled with the potentially horrendous human costs of error, attitudes toward casualties can be expected to remain uppermost in the thinking of Israeli policy-makers and strategic planners toward the next decade. Israeli decisions pertaining to preemption, preventive war and the conduct of war will continue to be affected by casualty expectations, with the nature of future conflict allowing far less flexibility than in the past.

Changing Economic Realities

For the first time since the 1973 war, there are reasons to be optimistic about the future of the Israeli economy. Government policies of the past several years have managed to stabilize an economy that seemed to be out of control. In 1984 the annual rate of inflation reached 450 percent but it dropped to only 16 percent in 1987. Similarly, foreign reserves in 1987 were at their highest levels ever, over $5 billion. If the government is able to maintain sound economic policies, real growth rates of 3-5 percent could be sustained for the next few years.

At least some analysts believe that if current trends continue and if plausible forecasts about the economy are correct, the Israeli economy may undergo a basic transformation during the next decade. The high-technology infrastructure will continue to grow and will become a dominant sector of the economy. This process will be facilitated by the Free Trade Agreement negotiated between the United States and Israel and the rapid increase in bilateral trade between the two countries. This should counter unfavorable trends: agriculture, rendered less profitable by the entry of Spain and Portugal in the European Common Market; tourism, subject to the threat of terrorism; and American aid, expected to decline in real dollar terms by inflation and likely Congressional and Administration action.

Following the 1982 Lebanon War, the Israeli government made a decision to hold defense spending to a constant proportion of current gross national product – around 16 to 18 percent. Heavy cuts in defense spending were made – over 20 percent in real terms. Further reductions in the proportionate size of the defense budget are expected should there be marked growth in the economy in the future. This policy was dictated by economic necessity, but was made possible by a favorable strategic balance.

By 1987, domestic defense spending had declined to levels comparable to those of before the 1973 war. According to one estimate, Israel's 1986 defense budget was $4.3 billion in a gross national product of $26.5 billion. Thus, defense spending was 16 percent of gross national product, the lowest level since 1966 (when it was 10.4 percent).[11] Nevertheless, the per capita defense burden on the average Israeli will remain much heavier than that carried by the citi-

---

[11] Aharon Levran and Zeev Eytan, *The Middle East Military Balance 1986* (Boulder, Colorado: Westview Press, 1987), p. 259.

zenry of any other Western country, although the burden will be lighter than at any time in the past two decades. According to the U.S. Arms Control and Disarmament Agency, in 1984 Israel spent $1,721 per capita on defense, the fourth highest of any country in the world. By comparison, the United States (ranked seventh) spent only $968, and France (ranked sixteenth) only $393.[12]

At the same time that Israel has reduced its domestic defense spending, it seems increasingly unlikely that the United States will be able to maintain current levels of aid to Israel, which include $1.8 billion in military assistance and $1.2 billion in economic aid. Even if aid levels are not reduced, the real value of the assistance will decline as a result of inflation. Should inflation in the United States average 5 percent per year, by 1995 the real value of Israel's military aid will drop from $1.8 billion to only $1.26 billion, a decline of 30 percent.

A major focus of industrial development will be connected with the country's security needs, and defense related work will continue to require a significant portion of the industrial labor force (currently 16 percent). This high-tech industrial base will bolster the civilian economy and at the same time meet the demands of national security.

A great deal will depend on the health of the Israeli economy. A resumption of steady economic growth would make it possible either to increase defense spending without increasing the portion of the economy devoted to defense or to further lower the burden of defense. Thus, if real growth through 1995 were to average 3 percent per year, the overall size of

---

[12] Arms Control and Disarmament Agency, *World Military Expenditures and Arms Transfers 1986* (Washington, D.C.: Government Printing Office, 1987), p. 17.

the economy would increase by 25 percent. Such an increase could significantly ease the current tight restrictions on defense spending.

The Post-Lavi Era

The September 1987 cancellation of the Lavi fighter project, after seven years of development and an investment of $1.5 billion (mainly in American aid money), was a function of economic and operational considerations. Though the cancellation raised some very serious questions about the future capabilities of Israel's military industrial complex, most observers believe that the decision ultimately will not have a profound long-term effect on Israel's ability to maintain its qualitative edge. On the contrary, cancellation of the project will make available funds for a wide range of developments better suited to the challenges of the future battlefield. The cancellation of the Lavi will serve to resuscitate branches of the armaments research and development complex, such as Rafael, the Weapons' Development Authority, that were severely curtailed by the concentration of resources in Lavi development.

The most obvious and immediate consequence of the decision to cancel the Lavi has been to force a complete re-thinking of the composition of the IDF of the 1990s. The course of future developments is not clear-cut. There are profound differences of opinion within Israel's defense establishment as to the optimal future mix of the IDF. Some advocate a small but technologically superior army, while others call for a more traditionally-organized force. The course eventually decided upon, will probably fall between these two approaches. Israel cannot economically afford to maintain its current order of battle and revolutionize it at the same time. Conversely, it cannot afford to put all its eggs into an unproven technological basket, without having adequate forces to hold the line if technology should fail.

Regardless of the final mix, it is generally agreed that in the 1990s the IDF will have a reduced order of battle, and that the reduction will be across the board. A smaller standing army, in the face of a more destructive, accurate and immediate threat, however, raises many questions on both the operational and strategic levels. The strategic implications, specifically the impact on deterrence and preemption, will be discussed in the following section.

On the operational level, it is clear that a smaller order of battle will necessitate greater adaptability, and that this will require a high degree of integration, centralized command and control, real-time intelligence capabilities, and advanced battle management techniques. There are risks inherent in the selection of a highly centralized system, since if one part breaks down the operation of the whole could be jeopardized.

Accordingly, Israel will still find it necessary to enable its forces to operate in a relatively autonomous fashion. This need has been magnified by the changing role of the Air Force, since the ground forces will have to anticipate fighting the crucial first two days of a conflict without close air support. Nor will the Air Force be able to guarantee that the reserve call-up process will take place without enemy interference. The growing first-strike capabilities of potential adversaries will require significant additional investment in passive defensive measures. Airfields and equipment storage sites will have to be hardened further, alternative military facilities (such as ports, airfields, and bridges) will have to be built, and civil defense facilities expanded.

The debate over the future force composition of the IDF in the immediate aftermath of the Lavi's demise was complicated further by industrial and political pressures for a "quick fix" to ameliorate the impact of the project's cancellation. These pressures were adamantly opposed by those in the defense establishment who wanted to pause and consider the wider implications of force development before making any decisions and before committing increasingly scarce resources to unsuited or unessential programs.

An example of this tension was found in attitudes in mid 1987 toward three programs favored by the United States: an antitactical ballistic missile (ATBM) system, the Saar V missile boat project, and the acquisition of new submarines. The United States had expressed an interest in joint development projects in all three cases, making them highly attractive to the political-industrial echelons. Defense planners, however, challenged the wisdom of participation in any of these three systems, and considered them a potential waste of resources. The ATBM was a defensive, reactive system, and thus a single purpose system not adaptable for other missions. The Saar V was considered by all branches of the planning staff (other than the navy) to be a potential floating Lavi, providing little that upgrading the Saar IV could not achieve. Similarly, the acquisition of more submarines had slid very low on the list of military priorities.

What illustrates this example, other than the friction it displays between the political-industrial echelons and those responsible for long-term military planning, is the rapidity with which Israeli force-mix concepts are changing. In early 1987, both the missile boats and the submarines were perceived benefits of the Lavi's cancellation, but by August they had been dropped from the mainstream discussion. They had been replaced by new generation stand-off and brilliant munitions, enhancements to existing systems, new C^3I systems, and other initiatives considered to be force multipliers. Although it is likely that Israel will cooperate with a European-American effort to develop antitactical ballistic missile systems, the rationale for participation will be industrial, scientific, and economic. More important than the military benefits will be the potential technological spinoffs expected to result, and it is unlikely that ATBM will be a core element of the IDF's order of battle through the mid-1990s.

The debate over the future composition of the IDF is still in its very early stages. The array of choices, the doctrinal and economic implications of rapidly changing technologies, and the unclear nature of the potential threat have combined to add new degrees of uncertainty to the decision-making process. Internal Israeli political and industrial considerations, and the state of Israeli-American relations will further complicate matters. Notwithstanding the uncertainties, there were clear indications that:

- initially the force structure would be based essentially on those elements already part of the order of battle, but that this would gradually change as new types of systems enter service;

- platform enhancement should take precedence over platform procurement wherever possible;

- Israel should tend to favor purchase of foreign systems, especially from the United States, and local manufacturing should be limited to critical systems that cannot be procured abroad for economic or military reasons;

- Israel should concentrate its military production efforts in those areas where it has a clear edge over foreign suppliers;

- there must be tighter coordination between the

various industrial and research arms of the defense establishment, on the one hand, and
civilian industries, on the other;

- finally, the adoption of new generation technologies should be approached with caution
given the lack of experience in using them
and the possibility that they will have a
relatively short effective life-cycle.

The transition to the new generation of military systems will not be easy, and will require considerable
adjustment by the IDF, by the military industries,
and by political echelons. But if the approach is
handled correctly, Israel should be able to manage
the transition.

The Changing Role of the Israel Air Force

Whereas the fundamentals of Israeli doctrine remain unchanged, the means for achieving these
goals have undergone a revolutionary re-assessment
in recent years. The changes in means are a direct
function of the changing nature of the battlefield. As
Arab armies have acquired larger inventories of surface-to-surface and surface-to-air missiles, it became
clear to Israeli military planners that resources had
to be allocated more evenly between the ground and
air forces. No longer could the air force be given a
disproportionately large slice of the pie.

This change in attitude derived from a realization
that during the first days of a future war the Israel
Air Force (IAF) will be totally occupied with two
basic missions. First, it will be involved in defensive
operations to protect Israeli air space from enemy air
attacks, and second it will be engaged in offensive
operations against enemy air defenses and surface-
to-surface missile launchers. The air force's
preoccupation with such targets will stem from three

factors: the reduced number of aircraft available by the mid-1990s, the growing size and sophistication of the adversaries' air defenses, and a proliferation in the number of surface-to-surface missiles in the region. Especially important will be the destruction by the air force of surface-to-surface missile launchers. Israel does not have the ability to shoot down tactical ballistic missiles and such weapons pose a potential threat to vulnerable and crucial military facilities, and their employment could effectively hinder Israel's ability to conduct an orderly call-up of its reserves.

Equally important, the ability of the IAF to provide close air support for the ground forces was challenged by studies of the use of air power during the 1982 Lebanon War. Even though Israel had total air superiority, when using conventional bombs an average of three aircraft sorties were needed to kill a single Syrian tank. At the same time, it was evident that the chances of Israeli aircraft accidentally hitting friendly troops were unacceptably high. In one incident, 22 Israelis were killed when aircraft accidentally attacked an Israeli armored column. Such "friendly" kills can be expected to be much higher in any future conflict where enemy missiles will force Israeli attacks to be executed from greater heights and longer distances.

This change of thinking played an important role in the cancellation of the Lavi fighter project in the summer of 1987. The Lavi was intended primarily as a close air support aircraft, but by 1987 it had become clear that the IAF would not be able to perform the close support mission. Moreover, the defense budget could not support both the Lavi and the development of other necessary systems. Given the rapid pace of innovation in the area of designated munitions and robotic technologies, questions were being raised as to the advisability of using expensive and vulnerable aerial platforms to achieve what could be attained by other means.

As a result, the air force will not be able to provide any meaningful close support for the ground forces during the opening stages of a war. This necessitates a basic re-structuring of the means available to the ground forces to carry out their mission independently of the air force, primarily the acquisition of standoff guided weapons as integral elements of their order of battle.

During the 1990s, the missions of the IAF will include:

- air defense, to keep hostile aircraft out of Israeli air space;

- missile suppression, including destruction of enemy surface-to-surface and surface-to-air missile sites;

- interdiction, to prevent supplementary and logistic forces from reaching the battlefield;

- ground support, but only in the later stages of a conflict, once the primary threats have been negated.

To accomplish these missions, the IAF will be comprised of a mix of aircraft: F-16s with enhanced air-to-ground capabilities; F-15s, late model Kfirs; upgraded Phantoms; and some late model Skyhawks. There will be only limited additional purchases of new F-15 and F-16 aircraft. Of increasing importance will be the air force's combat support infrastructure. The platforms used for C^{3}I will remain the existing E-2C Hawkeye and Boeing 707s, supported by remotely piloted vehicles and static sensors.

The Problems Facing the Ground Forces

Assuming a Syrian attack on the Golan Heights, and accepting Israel's doctrinal truism that the IDF has to fight a fluid war confined to enemy territory, Israel's ground forces will be faced with the task of both stopping advancing Syrian forces and seizing the operational initiative. Only if the ground forces are able to seize and hold militarily critical terrain will it be possible to inflict a military defeat on its opponents. Thus, despite the importance of the air battle, it is the results on the ground that will ultimately determine the outcome.

The arena in which the fighting on the ground will take place is extraordinarily confined. The portion of the Golan Heights occupied by Israel is only 1,176 square kilometers. The disengagement line between the two countries is only about 80 kilometers long. Only about 25 kilometers separate the Syrian side of the disengagement zone from Israel's 1967 borders, and Damascus is only about 50 kilometers away from Israeli-held territory. Yet even these numbers exaggerate the amount of area available to the combatants. Because of geological formations, much of the ground in the area is relatively inaccessible to mechanized units. In reality, most critical fighting is likely to take place in an area of only about 240 square kilometers.

An Israeli counteroffensive through the Golan Heights into Syrian territory will have to penetrate multi-layered defenses including mines, physical obstacles, and heavily protected fortifications. The defense belt is defended by six armored and mechanized divisions equipped with nearly 2,000 tanks, hundreds of armored personnel carriers, and a large number of artillery pieces.

The density of combat units and fortifications on the battlefield is such that, Israeli front-line units will pay a high price in any attack, despite their military superiority. The high density will severely hamper the force maneuverability essential for the fluid style of warfare so central to Israeli doctrine. Thus, the classic means of avoiding frontal battles through reliance on the indirect approach, a concept closely associated with the IDF, will not be possible on the Golan Heights.

Nor will it be possible to bypass the Syrian defenses without high diplomatic and strategic costs. An Israeli attack through Jordan is not practical for diplomatic and military reasons. It would antagonize the United States, probably bring other Arab countries into the fighting, undermine Israel's peace with Egypt, and jeopardize the survival of a pro-Western regime that shares many common strategic interests with Israel. Equally important, a flanking maneuver though Jordan offers few military benefits. It would require a costly assault through the escarpment on the east bank of the Jordan Valley and the seizure of two large Jordanian urban areas, Irbid and Mafraq. Yet, the military advantages of such a move would be limited. Most of the border between Jordan and Syria is not trafficable, and the area that can be crossed lies adjacent to the Golan Heights, where Syrian defenses are at their strongest. A flanking movement through Lebanon will have many of the same implications, albeit to lesser degrees in most instances.

The ground forces are thus posed with three fundamental dilemmas in regard to a future conflict with Syria:

- they cannot count on close air support in the opening stages of conflict;

- they will not be able to execute a fluid, mobile, and dynamic battle due to the high force density in the theater of combat;

- the geographic indirect approach will not be a viable option.

To solve these problems, the focus of attention has shifted and an effort is being made to find technological solutions that will restore the initiative to the IDF and provide new opportunities for achieving operational surprise.

Among the systems being examined are:

- early warning systems;
- standoff weapons;
- robot munitions;
- kamikaze drones;
- attack helicopters;
- helicopters for target designation and deep force deployment;
- rockets and guided artillery to compensate for lack of air support;
- electronic interference with Syrian battle management;
- real-time intelligence capabilities;
- secure communications;
- all-weather, day and night, continuous fighting capabilities;
- high mobility in survivable vehicles;
- strategic weapons to force a swift cease-fire.

Among the systems likely to gain prominence in the near future are attack helicopters. Although they cannot replace the battle tank, since they cannot hold or seize ground, they can perform a variety of other missions essential to the conduct of offensive or defensive operations. On the defensive, they can provide a counterattack force able to respond rapidly to enemy penetrations into rear areas. On the attack, they can infiltrate enemy lines to ambush reinforcements or retreating enemy units, to attack lightly protected enemy positions, command posts, or air defense units, or to find and designate targets for long-range precision-guided munitions launched from other locations.

The restructuring of the IDF order of battle will be guided by a new five-year development plan that will advocate a combined arms approach in the widest of senses. Israel's current Chief of Staff, Lt. Gen. Dan Shomron, believes that the IDF has to be a small, highly mobile, highly sophisticated army, capable of responding to given threats with great ingenuity and speed.

Combined Arms

The further exacerbation of the quantity/force ratio between Israel and the confrontation states has given renewed life to the concept of force integration and force multiplication factors. The decision in the mid-1980s to establish a unified Ground Forces Command, after almost a decade of often heated debate is a first step in this respect. Adopting a slogan that "one plus one does not necessarily always equal two," the Ground Forces Command has assumed doctrinal responsibility for the infantry, armor, artillery, and engineers, in order to achieve maximum integration of ground elements. Doctrine is defined in close coordination with intelligence, air force (especially with the helicopter and attack helicopter units), and navy, and the means of battle are developed in coordination with the research and development branches of the defense establishment.

The combined arms concept is not confined only to ground forces. When equipment of value is developed for the air force, thought is immediately given to how it can be applied to other branches. When a new system is acquired for the artillery, a primary consideration is how it will enhance the IDF as a whole, not just the ground forces. An example of this was the use of artillery to assist in the destruction of the Syrian surface-to-air missile sites in June 1982. A vivid assessment of the high degree of force integration in the Israeli military is to be found in a Soviet analysis of Israel's method of attack on Syrian aircraft and air defenses during the 1982 Lebanese war:

> For carrying out these tasks, all the intelligence forces in organizational terms were unified by the Israeli Air Force Command into a single system which included the ground units, the air sub-units and the combat aircraft with special equipment on board. The ground units were to acquire reliable information on the organization of the air force and air defense control systems in the Arab states, the capability of onboard electronic equipment of the aircraft, the SAMs, the control and guidance points, their parameters of emission and interference to jamming as well as information on the nature of air force activities. These tasks were carried out in close cooperation with the airborne electronic intelligence and combat sub-units as well as the air force's combat units as can be seen, for example, from the fact that the Israeli fighters scrambled simultaneously (even 1 or 2 minutes before) the take-off of Syrian military aircraft. . . .

> For all elements of the air force electronic intelligence and suppression system, Israeli military industry developed specialized automatic control equipment, reconnaissance and jamming equipment, as well as ground-, sea- and air-based missiles which home on the radar emission. . . .

> The Israeli airborne intelligence and electronic combat sub-units were confronted with the tasks of systematically observing the operation of the Arab electronic systems and air defense and air force equipment and determining the effectiveness of the Israeli

strikes and the use of electronic combat equipment. For this purpose they employed Boeing-707s which were specially equipped with electronic equipment, helicopters as well as unmanned reconnaissance aircraft such as the Mastiff and Scout carrying radio and opticoelectronic intelligence equipment.[13]

The concept of combined arms that will underlie the future development of the IDF is consistent with its offensive doctrinal posture. Forces will be built to be active, rather than reactive. Backed by new technologies and highly centralized command and control functions, they will be used to create the circumstances for the exploitation of the line of least resistance despite the constraints of terrain and enemy force density.

Israeli Responses to the New Technologies

There are six measures required to ensure that the Israeli defense establishment will be able to take advantage of the new technologies.

1. The Israeli military will have to be constantly alert to new developments and maintain a high degree of innovation. Even the most successful institutions find it difficult to maintain flexibility and creativeness over long periods of time. There is considerable danger that overconfidence, ignorance, or mistaken judgments could at some time cause a failure to adapt to new developments. This happened in the period before the 1973 war, and it could

---

[13] S.V. Seroshtan, "Local Wars," *Voyenno-Istoricheskiy Zurnal*, No. 3, 1986, as translated by U.S. Joint Publication Research Service, "Electronic Combat in Local Wars in Near East," UMA-86-047, p. 70.

happen again.

2. Israel will require access to new technologies and the technical infrastructure to exploit them. This has two implications. There will have to be continued technology transfers to Israel from the United States and elsewhere. In addition, continued development of the defense industries will be essential. Since the defense industries will have to adapt to the emergence of new technologies and new technical possibilities, the levels of expertise will have to grow beyond present capabilities. Without a healthy defense industrial sector, Israel's military advantage could disappear.

3. In order to minimize the prospect of a surprise attack, Israel will have to continue to invest heavily in a comprehensive intelligence collection system to provide real-time information on the activities of potentially hostile forces. This will require additional acquisitions of electronic sensors, data fusion systems, and secure command, control and communications links. New sensor platforms will be required, including high-altitude, long-endurance, low-observable, remotely-piloted vehicles, to ensure continuous monitoring of activity deep in enemy territory. New sensors will be needed, including long-range ground surveillance radars and enhanced electro-optical systems.

4. The Israeli military will need to invest in systems that maximize the battle effectiveness of military forces. Although this may make it possible to reduce the size of the regular forces, the primary requirement will be to ensure that they have the fighting power to respond to an unexpected attack during the opening hours of a war while reserve units are being mobilized. If possible, the weapons should enable pre-emptive spoiling operations against enemy forces poised to mount a surprise attack. Military forces usually are extremely

vulnerable as they prepare to attack, making spoiling attacks of this type extremely effective.

5. Israel will have to emphasize technologies and operational methods that keep casualties to a minimum. Israel has done innovative work in this area in the past, especially in tank protection systems and protective gear for individual soldiers, and these efforts will have to be expanded in the future. New structural materials will have to be exploited to create new protective systems to counter new generation weapons.

6. The military will have to continue to attract and keep high-class manpower, despite lucrative inducements from private industry. It will also be necessary to maintain an ongoing relationship between the IDF and the country's high school and university systems, thus maintaining a balance between the IDF's qualitative manpower needs and the demands of new technologies.

4: The Transfer of Advanced Technology Weapons to the Middle East

Sophisticated systems using new military technologies inevitably will appear in the arsenals of Middle Eastern military forces during the next decade. Past experience suggests that every country in the region will try to acquire advanced technology systems, and that they will be able to find suppliers willing to provide such equipment -- the United States, Western Europe, and the Soviet Union. Even Egypt and Israel, which are now able to manufacture their own munitions still rely on overseas suppliers for a substantial portion of their new equipment, and especially of the most sophisticated systems.

The growing size and sophistication of arms industries in the region, suggest that it may be possible in the future for Middle Eastern countries to build advanced technology systems indigenously. Although there are limits to the capabilities of all these arms industries, most countries now have the ability to modify equipment that was obtained elsewhere, and some can design and build totally new systems. Nevertheless, military forces in the Middle East will remain dependent on imported high technology equipment. Even if they are able to manufacture some sophisticated systems, they will remain dependent on the transfer of underlying technologies from the United States, Western Europe, or the Soviet Union.

This dependence on foreign systems and technology, though moderated by domestic arms production, means that the character of the future battlefield in the Arab-Israeli conflict will be determined in part by the nature of the world arms trade in the coming years.

Technology Transfer to the Middle East

During the past fifteen years, the Middle East has been the world's largest arms market and during the early 1980s it accounted for 40% of the world's trade in munitions.[1] Much of the equipment acquired has been of considerable sophistication, testimony to the fact that there are countries willing to meet the regional demand for advanced weaponry. Most arms manufacturers have powerful economic incentives to export munitions, and many have diplomatic or military reasons as well. Because so many countries now build and export military equipment, it is usually possible for a buying country to find a supplier willing to provide particular types of systems.

Recent events in the Middle East clearly demonstrate the ease with which it is possible to obtain specific military systems, even if some supplying

---

1 U.S. Arms Control and Disarmament Agency, *World Military Expenditures and Arms Transfers 1986* (Washington, D.C.: Government Printing Office, 1987), pp. 101, 103.

countries are reluctant to sell them. Although the Soviet Union refused to supply Iraq with a nuclear reactor capable of producing the fissionable material needed to make atomic weapons, the French were perfectly willing to step into the breach and sell the necessary equipment. The refusal of the United States to sell Jordan advanced F-16 fighters was followed by offers from the Soviets to sell MiG-29s, from the French to provide Mirage 2000s, and from the British to supply Tornado fighter-bombers. Despite international efforts to impose an arms embargo, during the past seven years more than two dozen countries have sold munitions to Iran, including sources as diverse as Israel and Syria, Britain and North Korea, Switzerland and Libya.[2]

Even the United States and the Soviet Union, which often have an interest in limiting the transfer of sophisticated weapons, have contributed substantially to the proliferation of advanced systems in the Middle East. The Soviet Union has on occasion shown restraint, and has even developed less advanced weapons variants intended solely for export. Recently, however, it has demonstrated readiness to export more sophisticated, systems.

They have supplied Syria with SA-5 missiles, MiG-29 fighters, SS-21 missiles, air-launched antiradiation missiles, artillery cluster munitions, and Sepal antiship missiles. Syria also has received Soviet remotely piloted vehicles and recent reports indicate that Syrian tanks are being equipped with

---

[2] Details are taken from Aharon Levran and Zeev Eytan, *The Middle East Military Balance 1986* (Boulder, Colorado: Westview Press, 1987), pp. 115-116 and 237-238 for Iran, and pp. 153-154 for Jordan.

reactive armor provided by the Soviet Union.[3] Iraq has been provided with MiG-29 fighters, Su-25 attack aircraft, and possibly SS-21 missiles.[4] According to the U.S. Department of Defense, the Soviet Union has provided Libya with SA-5 missiles and the Senezh air defense command and control system, and other sources indicate that a new laser-guided version of the SA-6 missile was among the equipment captured by Chad from Libya in 1987.[5] Su-24 strike aircraft were supplied in early 1989.

Similarly, despite restraints induced by congressional pressures and technology transfer control regulations, the United States has sent a considerable amount of sophisticated military equipment to the Middle East. F-4E Phantom II fighters were sold to Iran and Israel in the 1960s, F-14 fighters to Iran and F-15 fighters to Israel and Saudi Arabia in the 1970s, and AWACS airborne early warning aircraft to Saudi Arabia in the 1980s. Modern missiles also have been sold, even though some proposed sales (like the IIR Mavericks intended for Saudi Arabia) were held up by Congressional opposition.

Even if the superpowers were to stop transfers, it would only slow down the spread of sophisticated weapons, with a growing number of capable arms industries throughout the world willing to export for the right price. Typical of this new generation of

---

[3] The London *Sunday Express*, December 6, 1987.

[4] Levran and Eytan, *Middle East Military Balance 1986*, pp. 254-255.

[5] U.S. Department of Defense, *Soviet Military Power 1987* (Washington, D.C.: Government Printing Office, 1987), p. 139.

suppliers is Brazil.[6] The Brazilians manufacture a variety of highly efficient weapons, including artillery rockets and armored cars. Some Brazilian systems, like the Astros II artillery rocket, are superior to those available from the major arms suppliers.[7] In addition, countries like Brazil often act as conduits for equipment made in Western countries. Many Brazilian systems incorporate Western components, such as gun turrets, and sometimes whole systems are used outright, like the Fireguard radar artillery used with the Astros II.

Countries with access to Western technology, like Egypt, Iraq, Israel, Jordan and Saudi Arabia, can readily obtain a wide range of European and American systems. As a result, Saudi Arabia and Israel can maintain inventories of guided weapons that would be the envy of most NATO countries. Saudi Arabia provides an especially interesting example of technology proliferation. The United States has supplied F-15 fighters, AIM-9L Sidewinder and AIM-7F Sparrow air-to-air missiles, AWACS airborne early warning systems, KE-3 tanker aircraft, Harpoon antiship missiles, Paveway II laser-guided bombs, and Maverick air-to-surface missiles. In addition, the United States has provided elaborate naval and air force command and control systems. France

---

[6] A good summary is provided by H.M.F. Howarth, "Brazil's Defense Industry: ambitious and fast growing," *International Defense Review*, September 1985, pp. 1413-1427.

[7] The Astros II using the SS-60 rocket has a range of 68 kilometers, double that of the U.S. Army's MLRS. The distinctive price/performance position of the Astros II is discussed in "Artillery Rocket Systems: A Unique Market," *Military Technology*, September 1987, p. 29. The Astros II has recently started to face competition from the Chinese Type 83, a 40-kilometer-range rocket intended solely for export.

has sold Saudi Arabia F-2000 frigates, Otomat antiship missiles, Shahine surface-to-air missiles (developed especially for Saudi Arabia), R-550 Magique air-to-air missiles, and helicopter-launched AS-15TT antiship missiles. Britain has sold Tornado interceptors and strike aircraft, JP-233 runway cratering munitions, and possibly Alarm antiradiation missiles.[8]

The quality of the munitions available to the Royal Saudi Air Force is equal to the best found in NATO countries in West Europe, and superior to most of them. The Saudis have better planes, equipped with better air-launched munitions (including laser-guided bombs and television-guided missiles) in quantities that are rarely available to NATO countries. Indeed, Saudi Arabia has sufficient munitions to fight a war lasting 60 days, which no NATO country would be able to do.[9] Similarly, most Warsaw Pact countries would envy the air defense system that the Soviet Union has provided to Syria. Not only do the Syrians have greater numbers of missile batteries and self-propelled anti-aircraft guns, but they also have a more complete version of the integrated Soviet air defense system.[10]

The widespread availability of capable weapons is evident in the ease with which it is possible to obtain the helicopters and antiship missiles. It is possible to

---

[8] Levran and Eytan, *Middle East Military Balance 1986*, pp. 338-344.

[9] *Aviation Week & Space Technology*, February 13, 1984, p. 27, notes that the Saudis wanted to obtain a 60 day supply of air-to-ground munitions for their F-5 fighters.

[10] Soviet shipments of air defense equipment are discussed in greater detail in Chapter 2.

legally obtain modern helicopters from many sources other than the two superpowers. Aerospatiale in France, Agusta in Italy, MBB in Germany, Spain or Indonesia, or Westland in Britain are all able to supply helicopters of modern design. It is also possible to acquire them illegally. The North Koreans were able to obtain American-made Hughes 300 and 500 helicopters a few years ago with few problems.[11]

Similarly, antiship missiles are available from many countries. France, Italy, Norway, Britain, the People's Republic of China, and Israel export them. Middle Eastern military forces currently operate at least nine different antiship missiles: Italian-made Otomats (Libya, Egypt, and Saudi Arabia), French-made Exocets (Iraq, Kuwait, and Libya), French-made AS-15TT missiles (Saudi Arabia), American-made Harpoons (Israel, Egypt, and Saudi Arabia), Soviet-made SS-N-2/SSC-3 Styx of various types (Egypt, Libya, and Syria), Soviet-made SSC-1B Sepals (Syria), Chinese-made HY-2 (Iran and Egypt), Soviet-made SSC-2B Samlets (Syria), and Israeli-made Gabriels (Israel).[12]

More significant than the ease with which it has been possible to acquire existing systems has been the ability of countries in the Middle East to find

---

[11] Stuart Auerbach, "Copter Shipments Detailed: Customs Reportedly Failed to Bar Sales to N. Korea," *Washington Post*, February 27, 1985, p. A2.

[12] This may not be a complete list. Levran and Eytan, *Middle East Military Balance 1986*, pp. 424-425, 446-447, also includes the Israeli-made Barak (Israel), the Italian-made Sea Killer (Iran), three different Soviet-made systems used by Iraq (AS-4 Kennel, AS-6 Kingfish, and possibly the Elix), and two additional Soviet missiles used by Egypt (AS-1 Kennel and AS-5 Kelt).

Western arms manufacturers willing to develop and build equipment designed to meet specialized requirements. Teledyne Ryan is developing the Scarab RPV for Egypt, a sophisticated reconnaissance vehicle with a range of 1,700 nautical miles that relies on satellite GPS signals for precise navigation.[13] An Italian company designed the Egyptian Skyguard air defense system, which integrates radars with surface-to-air missiles and anti-aircraft guns, and another has provided Egypt and Iraq with specially configured self-protection jamming pods for their fighter aircraft. Indeed, the Italians were willing to supply Iraq with pods for protection against American Hawk surface-to-air missiles used by the Iranians, despite technology control regulations that should have prevented such transfers.[14] A French company has designed two generations of Shahine surface-to-air missile for the Saudis.

The result of these conditions is that by the middle of the 1980s every Middle East country has been able to obtain substantial inventories of military hardware, despite dependence on external sources of supply. This experience suggests that so long as a high priority is placed on the acquisition of munitions, it will be possible to obtain them and that in the future it will be difficult to prevent proliferation of advanced technology military systems to the region.

---

[13] Bruce A. Smith, "New Vehicles Mark Teledyne Ryan's Strong Return to RPV Business," *Aviation Week & Space Technology*, November 30, 1987, pp. 53-55.

[14] On the Italian pods, see Aerospace Daily, January 31, 1983, p. 162, and Anthony Cordesman, "NATO C^{3}I: The Problem of Security," *Armed Forces Journal International*, December 1982, p. 56.

The Transfer of Advanced Technology Weapons

Although past experience suggests that advanced technology weapons will make their way to the Middle East with considerable rapidity, the new generation of military systems might follow a different pattern. The number of countries making the new types of equipment will be relatively small at first, probably limited to the United States, the Soviet Union, and certain Western European countries. Because so few countries possess the technology required to build many of the new systems, it will be harder to locate suppliers willing to provide them. The smaller suppliers that have emerged in recent years as major arms exporters, like China, Brazil, or Austria do not have the necessary technology, and will not be in a position to export high technology systems for some time.

The countries that do have the technology will have strong incentives to protect the secrets of their new systems. Especially in the United States and the Soviet Union it is generally believed that the new weapons have war-winning capability. Many of the advanced technology systems being developed in the United States are considered "black" programs, and sometimes not even NATO allies are given access to the technologies involved. Given such attitudes, it is difficult to believe that the United States will be ready to sell advanced technology systems. It will take some time before the systems are exported, and even then it is likely that export versions will have sub-systems or computer software less capable than the standard versions.

In addition, advanced technology systems being developed in the United States, West Europe, or the Soviet Union are designed to deal with specific operational and environmental conditions. There is no evidence that anyone is making systems optimized for use in the radically different climate of the Middle East. Thus, certain kinds of infrared sensors that work perfectly well in a European environment may be less effective in hot desert conditions. Hence, even if it is possible to obtain the most sophisticated foreign systems, they may be less effective than systems optimized for local conditions.

Nevertheless, it is difficult to believe that such systems will not be adapted and made available to countries in the region. The commercial motive will inevitably overcome security considerations, certainly among the West European countries if not in the Soviet Union or the United States. European exporters, like France and Italy, have in the past shown no compunction about selling sophisticated systems despite technology export controls, and there is no reason to expect them to act any differently in the future. In addition, the technologies required to build advanced sensor systems, "brilliant" munitions, and deep-strike weaponry will be acquired by additional countries and it is almost inevitable that they will export the hardware to the Middle East. (For a further discussion of these weapons systems please see the appendix, page 185).

Indigenous Military Production

The past decade has seen a considerable growth in the size and sophistication of arms industries in the Middle East. Israel's is the most advanced, but virtually all Arab countries also have encouraged the growth of indigenous military production.

The capabilities of Israel's arms industry are too well known to require much elaboration. Less well understood is the extent to which the defense industries form an integral part of Israel's military. These companies provide the IDF with unique types of hardware; make it possible for Israel to quickly and inexpensively modify existing equipment by adding additional capabilities or correcting existing weaknesses; give the Israeli military a quick reaction capability to cope with the appearance of new enemy systems, and make it possible for Israel to field surprise weapons.

Israel can develop and field equipment not available elsewhere. These systems are not characterized simply by their technological sophistication, although they can employ relatively advanced technologies. Rather, they tend to involve applications where Israel has perceived a vital need that is not adequately recognized elsewhere. Systems of this type include the reactive armor fitted to Israel's foreign-made tanks, mini-RPVs, and upgraded tank ammunition. In all these cases, Israel simply made use of technologies developed by other countries (the technology for the reactive armor came from Germany; the mini-RPV and ammunition technology came from the United States). But the Israelis developed fieldable systems, while foreign countries allowed the technology to remain unexploited.[15]

This ability is a direct result of the close cooperation between the scientists and engineers who develop new equipment, and the soldiers who must use it on the battlefield. Because Israeli scientists and engineers are familiar with advances in technology as well as with operational military requirements, they often take advantage of promising developments that are ignored elsewhere. Similarly, military officials can alter operational requirements when they are alerted to the availability of new

---

[15] See W. Seth Carus, *U.S. Procurement of Israeli Defense Goods and Services* (Washington, D.C.: American Israel Public Affairs Committee, 1984), pp. 16-18.

technologies to solve existing problems that could not be dealt with using the old ones.

Israel has the technical and industrial infrastructure required to design and develop advanced systems indigenously, unlike other countries in the Middle East. It also has access to a considerable amount of Western technology, both American and West European, through joint research and development agreements with governments and defense manufacturers. This means that although Israel will not be able to obtain full access to complete Western systems or technology in many key areas, due primarily to controls over technology transfer, it should be able to provide its military forces with a mix of American-made and locally-developed advanced systems. As a result, during the 1990s the Israeli military will possess a growing variety of advanced weapons, sensors, and integrated systems.

The arms industries of the Arab countries are not as sophisticated as Israel's, and they will not be able to rely on them as a source of advanced systems. The following generalizations can be made about the state of Arab arms industries:

- The capabilities of Arab arms industries are growing, and the sophistication of the systems they produce is increasing.

- Arab countries cannot produce advanced technology weapons, a state of affairs expected to continue for the foreseeable future. Egypt is a partial exception, since it can build some relatively complex systems, including surface-to-air missiles, armored vehicles, and radars.

- Arab countries are dependent on foreign research and development for locally-manufactured military equipment of any sophistication. Most of the advanced equipment made in Egypt has been produced with considerable assistance from foreign technicians. In many cases, the

> equipment is merely assembled in Egypt, and the complicated design and manufacturing processes take place in the country of origin.

The situation varies considerably from one Arab country to the next, however, and these differences will have an impact on the Arab-Israeli military balance.

The most sophisticated arms industry in the Arab world is in Egypt. The Egyptians can assemble training aircraft and light attack aircraft, like the French Alpha Jets or the Brazilian Tucanos, and they can manufacture missiles and rockets. Egypt has initiated development of a variety of new military systems, including a joint surface-to-surface missile with Iraq.[16] Nevertheless, Egypt remains heavily dependent on foreign design expertise for its locally-made systems. Much of it is built under licence, including the British Swingfire antitank missiles and the American TPS-63 air search radars. Even when the design is uniquely Egyptian, it generally appears that foreign design teams played a major role in the development of the system. Thus, it appears that Italian experts helped design the 122mm Saqr rocket artillery, French technicians did the reverse engineering for the Ain al-Saqr surface-to-air missile (a version of the Soviet SA-7), and French and Italian firms are offering competing designs for a new self-propelled 23mm anti-aircraft gun system. Despite diminishing dependence on imports of arms, reliance on foreign design remains substan-

---

[16] For a survey of the Egyptian arms industry, see Mohammad El-Sayed Selim, "Egypt," pp. 123-156, in James Everett Katz, *Arms Production in Developing Countries* (Lexington, Mass.: Lexington Books, D.C. Heath and Company, 1984).

tial.[17]

Iraq now makes cluster munitions, small arms, and ammunition, but it is largely dependent on foreign expertise. Chile built and helps operate the cluster bomb assembly facility, and the most difficult component, the bomblets, are apparently manufactured in Chile.[18] In other areas they rely on Soviet, French, and Yugoslav assistance. The most sophisticated part of the Iraqi arms industry are its nuclear and chemical programs.[19]

Jordan remains without a substantial arms industry, but is slowly beginning to acquire the ability to modify some of its existing systems. Exemplifying this trend is the King Faisal tank modification facility in Jordan. This plant takes obsolescent Centurion tanks and converts them into upgraded Tarik tanks. The tanks are given new diesel engines and transmissions, and an array of electronic systems expected in modern battle tanks: digital fire control computers, laser rangefinders, and night sights. In this fashion, the Jordanians can produce new tanks equal in effectiveness to new M-60A3 battle tanks that cost a great deal more. All the components needed for the conversion were obtained in the United States

---

[17] "Cairo Emphasizes Local Production," *International Defense Review*, February 1985, pp. 213-222, and Robert Bailey, "Egypt: defence show gives military industry a boost," *Middle East Economic Digest*, November 21, 1987, p. 11.

[18] *Defense and Foreign Affairs*, August 1985, p. 1.

[19] Levran and Eytan, *Middle East Military Balance 1986*, pp. 89-90, 249.

or Europe.[20]

Significantly, Syria has a very small arms industry. So far as is known, Syrian production capabilities are limited to the manufacture of some types of ammunition. They are also capable of making simple modifications to existing equipment. Prior to the 1973 war they converted some of their old T-34 tanks into self-propelled field artillery by replacing the turrets with 122mm guns.[21] Similarly, in recent years the Syrians have been able to upgrade existing tanks by adding laser rangefinders and improved night vision equipment acquired from other countries.[22] Only in the area of chemical warfare have the Syrians developed a local infrastructure of any importance. They manufacture nerve gas, and have developed a chemical warhead for their Soviet-supplied Scud missiles.[23]

Military leaders in the Arab world appear to have strong incentives to expand and modernize their defense industries. In many cases they appear to believe that such enterprises are essential to their national security, and that even if not cost-competitive, the strategic benefits of indigenous arms production far outweigh the economic costs. This attitude is reflected in the remarks of 'Abd al-Halim Abu Ghazalah, Egypt's former Minister of Defense and War

---

[20] Anthony Cordesman, *Jordan Arms and the Middle East Balance* (Washington, D.C.: Middle East Institute, 1983), p. 63.

[21] Joseph S. Bermudez, Jr., "Syrian T-34/122 self-propelled gun," *Jane's Defence Weekly,* September 15, 1985, pp. 468-470.

[22] Levran and Eytan, *Middle East Military Balance 1986,* p. 178.

[23] Levran and Eytan, *Middle East Military Balance 1986,* pp. 180-181.

Production.

> It is scientifically known that whichever coun-
> try possesses the superior technological capabil-
> ity in the developmental and industrial fields
> also possesses the elements of deterrence and
> free political decision-making. It is obvious
> that the country which imports its weapons
> from another country is affected in its decision-
> making by the exporting country. Therefore,
> we have plans to create a military industry
> capable of providing the basics. This will
> enable Egypt to be self-reliant in the event of a
> crisis and or whenever necessary.[24]

It is for such reasons that the Egyptians have laid
such stress on programs to enhance the sophistication of their arms industry, including plans to manufacture the American M-1 tank in Egypt. Other
countries in the Arab world also are striving to expand their defense industries and increase the
sophistication of the equipment that they can develop.

Unlike Israel, however, Arab military industries
will not be able to manufacture advanced technology
systems. No Arab country has the scientific and engineering base to support such efforts. Although the
sophistication of the products of Arab arms industries
will grow over time, they will not be able to design
or produce state-of-the-art systems. To some extent it
may be possible to hire foreign technicians or
companies to assist in the development of sophisticated equipment, an approach adopted with considerable success by South Africa, but this approach
works only if the companies doing the hiring have

---

[24] Interview on *Cairo Domestic Service* (in Arabic) on October 6,
1987, as translated by FBIS, *Daily Report: Near East and South
Asia*, October 7, 1987, p. 5.

the management and technical expertise to exploit the foreign talent. The potential problems inherent in this approach are evident from Egypt's unsatisfactory attempts to employ German scientists in the 1950s and 1960s to create a modern arms industry. This suggests that even with the emergence of more capable defense industries in the Arab world, Arab military forces will remain dependent on foreign suppliers for high technology equipment.

High Technology Systems and the Arab-Israeli Confrontation

Even Israel, which has an advanced scientific and technical infrastructure, will depend on technologies and devices manufactured in the United States and elsewhere. Thus, to a large extent, the ability of Middle Eastern countries to obtain sophisticated military systems will depend on the willingness of external suppliers to provide it.

Despite this dependence on foreign suppliers, the capabilities of national defense industries will be critical. It will be much easier to obtain sub-systems than to acquire complete advanced systems, so that a country that can take advantage of technologies obtained elsewhere will be able to develop and field complete systems long before they are available from foreign suppliers. For this reason, Israel's ability to work with advanced technology systems will give it a decided advantage over countries like Syria that lack such capabilities.

This state of affairs suggests that there will be a gap between the time that Israel acquires sophisticated new weapons and the time that they start appearing in Arab arsenals. Countries dependent on the Soviet Union for their military equipment, like Syria, may be particularly disadvantaged. Not only is the Soviet Union less capable of developing such systems than Western countries, because of technological weaknesses, but the Soviet Union has shown considerable reluctance to export highly sophisticated weapons critical to its own defenses. Hence, it appears that there is a "window of opportunity" through which Israel will have greater access to new-generation military systems.

(TABLE 5)
MIDDLE EAST ARMS IMPORTS
1974-1985

Year	Arms Imports ($ millions)	Total Arms Imports ($ millions)
1975	3,950	3,950
1976	5,845	9,795
1977	7,960	17,755
1978	9,040	26,795
1979	9,725	36,520
1980	9,885	46,405
1981	14,600	61,005
1982	16,610	77,615
1983	17,340	94,955
1984	18,060	113,015
1985	9,390	122,405
Total	**122,405**	

Source: Arms Control and Disarmament Agency, *World Military Expenditures and Arms Transfers 1986* (Washington, D.C.: Government Printing Office, 1987), p. 103. Note that the table includes all countries in the region (including Israel), and not just countries directly involved in the Arab-Israeli conflict.

5: New Technologies and the Economics of War

The economic costs of advanced technology military systems may place severe constraints on the ability of countries in the Middle East to obtain such equipment. These systems can be very costly, and are often significantly more expensive than the equipment being replaced. Many American experts believe that financial constraints will severely limit the acquisition of such systems by Western countries. This is even more true for developing countries. As one senior U.S. Air Force official noted, "some of the technological advances may become so very expensive that we will be on the verge of being unable to afford them."[1]

Manufacturing costs, are usually only a fraction of the total cost of a new system. In many cases,

---

[1] General Lawrence A. Skantze, as cited in Bruce D. Nordwall, "High Cost of Aircraft Avionics Threatens U.S. Defense Capabilities," *Aviation Week & Space Technology*, June 8, 1987, p. 81.

heavy research and development expenditures can equal the procurement costs of the weapon.[2] And this does not take into account training, maintenance and operation expenditures, or the cost of incorporating the new systems into an existing military infrastructure.

Economic Risks and Advanced Technology Systems

In many cases, the costs of high technology defense equipment appear to be growing faster than the growth in defense budgets, and are, as a consequence, placing heavy strains on these budgets. As Norman Augustine has noted, if present trends continue the cost of a single airplane in the year 2054 would equal the entire U.S. defense budget.[3]

The control of development, production, and acquisition costs has proven exceedingly difficult. Not untypical is the U.S. Army's Copperhead, a laser-guided artillery round that can be fired from standard 155mm howitzers. In 1975, it was estimated that it would be possible to acquire the Copperhead for

---

[2] A good example of the economic problems facing weapons developers is provided by the Aquila mini-RPV being developed by the U.S. Army. Growing unit costs forced the U.S. Army to reduce the number of Aquila systems to be built from 780 to 376, although the total amount to be spent on production was not changed. Development of the Aquila will cost $850 million, compared with anticipated production costs of $969 million, according to the General Accounting Office. See John D. Morocco, "GAO Warns of Potential Risks In Major New Weapons Programs," *Aviation Week & Space Technology*, April 13, 1987, p. 98.

[3] Norman Augustine, *Augustine's Laws* (New York: Penguin Books, 1987), p. 143.

only $3,500 per round, but by the time the first rounds were being bought the price had increased to $90,000, a result of unexpected design and production problems. Subsequent cost control measures, however, finally made it possible to bring the price down to about $35,000. There are countless similar examples.

When costs increase in such a dramatic and unpredictable way, it becomes almost impossible for military planners to accurately assess the ultimate cost-effectiveness of a system, making it difficult to judge the relative merits of proposed alternatives. Clearly, there is a difference between buying Copperheads at $3,500 and $90,000. At the lower price, it would have been possible to buy the Copperhead in large numbers, to use it freely in battle, and to accept less than perfect performance. At the higher price, however, the use of the Copperhead had to be restricted because fewer could be acquired and there was less room to tolerate performance failures. At $3,500 per round, the Copperhead could be used against low and medium-value targets, like trucks and armored personnel carriers. At $90,000 per round, its use would be restricted only to tanks and other very high-value targets. Although the Copperhead can still be used at the high price, it is highly possible that a decision may have been made to invest the resources in different ways had it been known how expensive the weapon was going to become.

Technological innovations do not necessarily result in higher costs, and in many cases procurement costs can be reduced. This is especially true for electronic systems, since new circuit designs are making it possible to produce devices that are cheaper to build and easier to maintain. The U.S. Air Force, for example, is able to acquire new inertial navigation systems for F-15s that cost less than the ones previously used, but that are nearly ten times more reliable.[4]

Another example is the Global Positioning System (GPS) now entering service with the U.S. Air Force. When the GPS program is completed, several thousand of the sets will be fitted in aircraft, ships, and ground vehicles to provide precise location information using satellite-generated signals. In 1979 it was expected that each set would cost $116,000 to purchase, but technological advances made it possible to cut the price to $47,000, a reduction of about 60%. It is likely that a new generation of GPS sets using more advanced integrated circuits will be smaller and still less expensive than the ones currently being acquired, making it possible to incorporate them into missiles and other expendable systems.[5]

The financial picture, thus, is not clearly defined. Some hardware is extremely expensive, and there is no way to make it cheaply. At the same time, however, other equipment is becoming less costly. Augustine has noted that:

> The point is not, of course, that new technology is inevitably more expensive than old technology; the opposite is often the case. But what happens is that, as has been noted, new technology opens vast new capability vistas which are then crammed into each new

---

[4] Ulsamer, "Down-to-Earth Concerns About Tactical Air," *Air Force Magazine*, April 1985, p. 64.

[5] See Philip J. Klass, "First Production GPS Receiver Delivered Ahead of Schedule," *Aviation Week & Space Technology*, September 21, 1987, pp. 93-101. The price cited is for the most capable and highest cost sets.

generation of a product.[6]

Thus, the state-of-the-art is pushed to the limits, and costs often climb rapidly.

Equipment Cost and Performance

Concentrating only on cost, however, gives an incomplete picture. Operational effectiveness also must be taken into account. In many circumstances, it is possible that a costlier weapon, because it is more effective, may be less expensive to use than a simpler alternative. This is illustrated by the example of the laser-guided bomb. When attacking point targets, a single laser-guided bomb has the potential effectiveness of hundreds of unguided "dumb" bombs. According to calculations made by Texas Instruments, a single laser-guided glide bomb costing $10,270 can have the same military effect as 200 manually-released bombs (costing $454,000) or 40 computer-released bombs (costing $90,800). This does not take into account the savings through fewer sorties and resulting lower aircraft attrition rates.[7] It is necessary to be careful when making such comparisons, however, since the real cost of using a smart weapon may be increased by the need to use highly sophisticated, relatively expensive weapons control systems. In such cases, the cost of the ordnance may be only a small part of the total acquisition cost of a weapon.

Similarly, there are highly expensive, sophisti-

---

[6] Augustine, *Augustine's Laws*, p. 140.

[7] These estimates were provided in undated promotional material published by Texas Instruments.

cated systems that have considerable operational utility and may be an essential part of any future military force. Antiship missiles costing up to $750,000, like the U.S. Navy's Harpoon, are generally considered reasonable investments, because of their considerable potential effectiveness in battle. The antiship version of the U.S. Navy's Tomahawk cruise missile is even more expensive, but the long range attack capabilities of the system are thought to justify its high cost. The reason such costly weapons are considered worth buying is that the targets that they are able to destroy are worth much more.

The same may be true in other circumstances where the cost-benefit margins are less self-evident. The U.S. Air Force buys expensive F-15 fighters, because their performance offers operational military advantages not provided by less costly aircraft. USAF planners believe that the overall gain outweighs the high costs that limit the number that can be acquired, a judgement shared by the Israeli Air Force. Similarly, the development and acquisition of a weapon like the AMRAAM, a fire-and-forget radar-guided air-to-air missile, will be expensive, but many air force officials (both in the United States and elsewhere) argue that the high cost will be worthwhile because of the high value of the targets that it can destroy.[8]

The problems of accurately predicting a system's battlefield effectiveness makes it difficult to estimate the quantities required to accomplish particular tasks. It is often assumed, for example, that the high kill-rates of sophisticated munitions will make it possible

---

[8] Many of the issues are reviewed by Walter Kross, *Military Reform: The High-Tech Debate in the Tactical Air Forces* (Washington: Government Printing Office, 1985), pp. 100-101, 103-104.

to use them in small numbers. This may not be true. The enemy may employ countermeasures that reduce effectiveness, or the weapons may be used under less than optimal circumstances. (These points are discussed in more detail in chapter 8). Thus, it is not unusual to find fighter pilots firing air-to-air missiles at enemy aircraft that are at the outer edge of the missile's performance envelope, where the kill probability is low, to take advantage of a fleeting opportunity to kill the enemy, to force the opposing pilot to maneuver in ways that may make possible a more successful follow-up attack, or out of incompetence. Moreover, soldiers often do not use weapons as originally intended by the designers and procurement bureaucracies. British infantry-men used Milan antitank missiles to attack bunkers during the Falklands War, a possibility not covered in planning data used to estimate likely consumption of antitank missiles.

There is no necessary clear-cut connection between cost and effectiveness. Many extremely expensive systems have only limited combat effectiveness, while simpler and less expensive systems can be highly effective when used under appropriate circumstances. Similarly, it is often possible to obtain substantial improvements in effectiveness through use of more expensive equipment.

The history of the U.S. Army's tank program during the past twenty-five years vividly illustrates this point. Through most of the 1960s, the United States Army bought M-60A1 tanks, which were armed with 105mm high velocity guns. Despite some weaknesses, these tanks proved to be extremely effective when used in combat by Israel during the 1973 war. This tank cost about $292,000 (in 1972 dollars). During the 1960s, however, the U.S. Army, developed a new version of the M-60, the M-60A2.

This new model was armed with a combined 152mm gun/missile launcher, which made it possible to fire antitank missiles through the gun, and a sophisticated fire control system. Even though the M-60A2 never worked properly and it was dropped from the inventory, it cost about $707,000 (in constant 1972 dollars), two and half times the price of an M-60A1.[9]

The same story was repeated when the Army attempted to develop a replacement for the entire M-60 family of tanks, the highly sophisticated XM-803. The XM-803 never worked properly, and was cancelled before development ended. The cost of the XM-803 was estimated at $700,000 (1972 dollars), or about the same as the M-60A2. Because of the failure of the XM-803, the Army had to rely on an upgraded version of the M-60A1, the M-60A3. Despite some problems, this new version performed well in the Israeli army in combat during the 1982 Lebanon fighting, even though it cost only $393,000 (1972 dollars). Although 33% more expensive than the M-60A1, the M-60A3 was 40% less costly than the other alternatives, and it also functioned quite well. The U.S. Army's new M-1 battle tank costs $507,000 (1972 dollars), about 30% more than the M-60A3. Although less expensive than the proposed XM-803, it is clearly the superior vehicle. Similarly, although it is more expensive than the M-60 series tanks, the U.S. Army argues that the improvements in capability, and

---

[9] These figures were taken from Seymour Deitchman, *Military Power and the Advance of Technology: General Purpose Military Forces for the 1980s and Beyond* (Boulder, Colo.: Westview Press, 1983), p. 235. The fire control system accounted for much of the difference in cost. The one on the M-60A1 cost $75,000, the one on the M-60A2 cost an estimated $250-300,000, the XM-803's was estimated at $323,000, the M-60A3's cost $75,000, and the M-1's cost $145-200,000.

especially in vehicle survivability, more than justify the price increase. This view is shared by the Israeli military, which spent comparable amounts to buy its roughly comparable Merkava battle tank. Israeli armor officers believe that experience in Lebanon demonstrated that the extra performance of tanks like the Merkava justifies their high cost. Thus, while an expensive weapon may be more effective than a cheaper one, the reverse is also possible.

Interactions of this type can result in changed perceptions of cost-effectiveness, further complicating force structure considerations. Alternative weapons may appear that fulfill particular roles at lower costs than current systems, or the cost of maintaining operational viability in the face of enemy weapons and countermeasures may be so great that the weapon ceases to be cost effective. It is possible for a weapon to become obsolete simply because the economic costs have become so large that alternative systems appear more attractive.

The Lavi and the Economics of Obsolescence

Economic and operational factors interacted to play a significant role in the ultimate demise of Israel's planned fighter-bomber, the Lavi. The Lavi was to provide close air-support for ground forces. To accomplish this mission, the plane had to be able to survive in a dense air-defense environment composed of large numbers of surface-to-air missiles and anti-aircraft guns of many different types. This meant that the Lavi had to have sophisticated self-protection electronic countermeasures to confound electronically-operated air defense systems. It also needed powerful engines so that the plane could pass through defended territory as quickly as possible, thus reducing exposure to enemy defenses. Other demands were a sophisticated radar and weapons delivery system so that targets could be acquired and attacked at a distance, requiring only a single pass over the target and at the same time allowing weapons release at a distance from densest part of the defenses. The plane also had to be able to carry such stand-off weapons. The result was a price of between $16 million (by conservative estimate) and may have cost as much as $23 million. Nor was it possible to reduce the cost of the plane, without lowering capabilities and survivability.

At the same time that operational considerations had made the Lavi expensive, technological advances were reducing the need for a close air-support aircraft. Sophisticated guided munitions could be delivered just as well from platforms costing far less. The possibility of developing ground-launched guided weapons, or longer-ranged air-launched guided weapons that could be released from low performance aircraft operating outside the effective range of air defenses, reduced the need for an expensive high performance aircraft. Indeed, to some extent the close air-support aircraft had become a liability. Any investment of resources in the plane meant less were available for other weapons.

An important change had taken place in the role of air power. During the 1970s and early 1980s, it was possible to acquire smarter and more powerful aircraft, like the F-16, that could deliver cheap iron bombs ("dumb" weapons) with considerable accuracy. Once the bombs became smarter, the advantages of the expensive plane began to disappear.[10]

Two conclusions are suggested by these observations. First, the costs of systems generally will increase in the future, as a result of the high research and development and production costs associated with the use of advanced technologies. At the same time, the financial risks will be relatively high, because of the difficulties of accurately predicting costs when using incompletely understood new technologies. These financial pressures will place constraints on the size a of military force relying heavily on advanced technology systems, and force it to minimize use of such systems.

Second, since technological innovations will alter the existing ratios of costs and benefits among competing systems, economic pressures will lead to shifts in the types of weapons systems. Some expensive ones will decline in importance and others will become more valuable as they assume the roles of the costly systems.

The high costs of future systems will place a tremendous managerial burden on defense establishments. Among the problems are inability to control expenditures, to find the available technologies to find the ones most appropriate to the given requirements, and to identify opportunities to develop inexpensive new types of systems. Perhaps such managerial considerations are the greatest single challenge of the new technologies.

---

10 This is primarily true in the Syrian-Israel context, since the combat arena is so small and it is possible to rely on systems without the range or flexibility of aircraft. If Israel's main enemy were Egypt or even Jordan, the ability of the fighter to cover large distances might have been more critical, and the decision to abandon the Lavi would have been harder to justify from an operational point of view.

Defense Economics and the
Syrian-Israeli Military Balance

The high costs of advanced weapons make it doubtful if a country like Israel can afford to rely heavily on advanced technology military systems. All that we know for certain is that the economic and operational costs of failure may be extremely high. Ultimately, economics will be central to the future of Israel's defense posture, and will have a critical impact on the interaction between high technology and the Arab-Israeli military balance.

Israel: Despite the improved health of the Israeli economy, reflected in the lower rates of inflation and the increases in foreign reserves, the decision of the Israeli government to limit the growth of defense spending means that military programs will have to be implemented within relatively severe economic constraints. Even if the economy continues to grow in real terms, defense budgets will not increase proportionately and military spending will remain tightly controlled. Hence, the Ministry of Defense will have difficulty in maintaining existing forces, funding research and development programs, and paying for new equipment.

Nor will it be possible to rely on American military aid, which is likely to decline in real terms in the coming years. Without cuts in aid, inflation will gradually erode its value. Growing research and development cooperation with the U.S. Department of Defense could be of major benefit in developing and maintaining new technologies. But such programs, as well as buying advanced technology systems off-the-shelf may be jeopardized by planned cuts in American defense spending, which may amount to more than $30 billion a year.[11]

For these reasons, the Israeli defense establishment will have to make hard choices between cutting the force structure, upgrading existing platforms, buying new equipment and developing new technologies. Assuming that current geostrategic conditions continue, and that the peace agreement with Egypt and the *de facto* peace arrangement with Jordan last, Israel will be able to save resources that otherwise would be needed to maintain forces to police and defend the Egyptian and Jordanian fronts. In addition, Israel's ability to develop and build many items locally should help reduce overall expenditure, because of lower labor and overhead costs. This is offset, however, by the limited number of weapons that Israel needs to produce to meet its own requirements, driving up unit costs. Effectively, the Lavi was killed when the number required dropped from 300 to 150, making the price of each plane so expensive that the project was no longer cost-effective.

Similarly, Israel gains a great deal by its ability to operate and maintain sophisticated equipment with only limited assistance from the United States. As a result, it usually costs Israel less to operate a particular system than Arab countries which have to rely on expensive foreign support. The differential is most evident in the cost of supporting F-15 fighters. Saudi Arabia spends far more on F-15 operation than Israel, largely because the Saudis must pay inflated

---

[11] Molly Moore, "Defense Department in Fiscal Retreat: 'Where Are We Headed?'," *Washington Post*, January 6, 1988, p. A21, notes that former Secretary of Defense Frank Carlucci has mandated cuts of $33 billion from the proposed fiscal year 1989 budget of $332 billion and that additional cuts are considered likely.

infrastructure support costs to American contractors, while Israel is able to rely on its own resources.

Israel also obtains considerable benefit from the ability of its defense industries to export equipment. This increases the size of production runs, driving down unit costs, and transferring to foreign customers part of the burden of supporting the defense infrastructure. Similarly, research and development programs paid for by foreign countries make it possible to maintain infrastructure that otherwise would have to be paid for from the defense budget.

Nevertheless, Israel will not find it easy to acquire advanced systems without encountering some severe economic problems. The Lavi experience suggests that the country may not have the necessary infrastructure to balance the economic consequences of research and development and procurement decisions, a weakness which could cause serious problems down the road. Similar problems may arise with the proposed antitactical-ballistic missile project, which the Israeli General Staff opposes, but is being supported by the Defense Ministry primarily for industrial and political reasons.

The problems of acquiring sophisticated systems will be eased by recognition that Israel cannot afford to build everything at home. Acquisition of foreign-made equipment, especially from the United States, will reduce economic risks, although it will require accepting systems not totally suited to Israeli requirements.

Syria: Syria's ability to fund a military modernization program will be determined by the health of its economy, by the costs of weapons, and by the amounts of financial aid received from abroad.

Experts on the Syrian economy believe that its fundamental structural problems are unlikely to be solved easily or in the short term, even by massive foreign assitance. The *Middle East Economic Digest* estimate appears to reflect a widely shared belief.

> Structural factors mean Syria's economic crisis will continue for some time. They include the inefficiency of the public sector and the distorting effect of the heavy defense burden.[12]

Only in the oil sector does it appear that conditions are improving. Newly discovered fields are allowing the Syrians to increase production, which should save $250 million a year in foreign exchange otherwise spent on petroleum imports. Although the 1981-1985 economic plan emphasized development in the agricultural sector, performance has not been up to expectation and the government ministers responsible for agriculture were among the officials removed from their posts in the recent cabinet shake-up. The ministers responsible for the industrial sector also were fired.[13] These moves are not expected to result in any fundamental changes in economic policy, and both agriculture and industry remain plagued by inefficiency, over-employment, poor management, and lack of foreign currency.

In the recent past, the Soviet Union has given Syria considerable amounts of financial assistance, mostly in the form of loans to pay for military hardware. Estimates of Syria's debt to the Soviet

---

[12] "Syria: grim times now, better prospects ahead," *Middle East Economic Digest*, April 11, 1987, p. 37.

[13] David Butter, "Parliament probe leads to Syrian cabinet shake-up," *Middle East Economic Digest*, November 7, 1987, p. 42.

Union range from $6-8 billion up to $15 billion.[14] There have been indications that the Soviets have demanded cash payment for equipment, but this may have applied to only specific acquisitions. Should the Soviet Union reduce its financial aid (or unfavorably change the repayment terms of loans), the ability of the Syrian military to acquire hardware will be reduced. Similarly, if the Soviets are willing to extend credits on easy terms, the Syrians will be able to continue to modernize their military forces. This is a major unknown, but it can be assumed will not provide the $1-2 billion a year required to continue the modernization programs into the 1990s. Nor will Syria be able to count on substantial increases in aid from other Arab countries. Although Syria was supposed to receive $1.85 billion per year by a decision of the 1978 Baghdad summit, currently only about $500 million per annum is being provided.[15] As the price of oil is not expected to increase substantially over its present level for some time, the Gulf states, mainly Saudi Arabia, will not have substantial pools of money for foreign aid.[16] Nevertheless, there are indications that Damascus

---

[14] Jack Redden, "Assad walking tightrope in talks this week with Kremlin," *Washington Times*, April 21, 1987, p. 9A, reports $6-8 billion; Andrew Borowiec, "Iran poses threat to stable Syrian financial situation," *Washington Times*, November 11, 1987, p. A9, cites an $11 billion figure; Kanovsky, "What's Behind Syria's Current Economic Problems?," p. 301, gives a figure of $11 to 15 billion.

[15] "Syria: grim times now, better prospects ahead," *Middle East Economic Digest*, April 11, 1987, pp. 36-37.

[16] James Tanner, "Oil Glut May Cause Price Slide By Spring," *Wall Street Journal*, November 25, 1987, p. 6, on the current state of the oil market.

could obtain significantly more aid from Arab Gulf states if it were to end its support for Iran, but Asad cannot be certain that higher levels would be maintained. Syria would have only limited leverage over the Gulf states once it actually changed policy, and there are other countries, like Egypt and Jordan, that are currently doing more to help the Gulf states and which have more substantial claims for assistance.

The weakness of the Syrian economy and the restricted foreign aid, plus the costs of maintaining current force structure and the presence in Lebanon make it difficult for Syria to afford additional expensive equipment, especially since they have had problems with absorbing existing systems. This is a reversal of the economic realities of the 1970s, which worked for the Arabs and against Israel. The Syrians attempted to expand their military machine in a period of economic contraction, and are now suffering the consequences. Indicative of this trend is the relative drop of defense spending in Israel as part of overall gross national product, compared to a corresponding growth in Syria.

This suggests that Syria will be able to acquire high technology military systems only when the costs are relatively modest. As we have seen, there will be categories of relatively inexpensive equipment. Only to this limited extent will Syria gain a substantial benefit from the new technologies. Although it can undertake equipment modification programs, it will be at a significant comparative disadvantage to Israel in this respect.

The Economics of the Israeli-Syrian Conflict

Both Israel and Syria have been forced to reduce their defense spending, and both are dependent on allies increasingly unable to maintain existing levels of military assistance. However, Israel has undertaken some of the reforms needed to revitalize its economy, whereas the Syrians have not yet been able to do the same. Similarly, despite its economic woes Israel has a relatively modern, Westernized economic infrastructure, whereas the Syrians have a more typically Third World economy.

It is evident that the Israeli military already has decided to invest in high technology systems. As the above discussion indicates, the economic uncertainties inherent in the exploitation of advanced technology systems makes this a high-risk strategy. Hence, if Israel is to retain its current edge in the military balance of power, the Israeli defense establishment must be able to effectively manage its high technology programs to make most efficient use of limited defense funds. Should Israel be able to meet the economic challenges presented by the new technologies, the Syrians will be presented with a serious economic problem. In order to cope with the new types of threats posed by Israel's new technology systems, the Syrians will be forced to make massive additional investments in new types of systems. This will force them to maintain a high level of spending on defense, drawn largely from internal sources, forcing them to make difficult choices between defense and civilian investments.

6: The Combat Effectiveness of the New Technologies

As the American military has come to rely to an increasing extent on advanced technology equipment, a debate has emerged in the United States over the effectiveness of such systems in battle. Those who advocate reliance on such systems are convinced that they have the potential to revolutionize the conduct of war. They believe that adoption of new systems can give a decisive military edge to a country with access to superior technology, making war prohibitively expensive for less advanced adversaries. In contrast, many critics doubt that high technology weapons will be as decisive as advocates sometimes suggest. They argue that the promise of sophisticated weapons is rarely fulfilled, because increasing complexity makes them difficult to use and excessively expensive.

This debate, however, fails to address a number of critical issues. The excessive focus on the technical strengths and weaknesses of hardware often leads to a tendency to ignore the human context within which the equipment is used. The qualities and capabilities of the men who fight wars, and who create and determine how the hardware is to be used, are at least as important as the capabilities of particular weapons and systems. Indeed, the two are inseparable: men must be considered in the context of the capabilities of the machines that they use, and the machines must be evaluated in the context of the men who must use them.

Debating the Combat Effectiveness of the New Technologies

The justification for adopting advanced technology military systems is that they provide armed forces with capabilities not available when using simpler systems. Unfortunately, such systems are often complex and based on technologies which are not always well understood, especially in Third World regions like the Middle East where technical expertise is often limited. As a result, integrating them into military forces can be counterproductive, since they can be unreliable, difficult to maintain, and harder to use – and sometimes more costly than existing systems. These problems are now generally recognized, by both advocates and critics of the use of advanced technology weaponry.[1]

There is, however, severe disagreement about

---

[1] For an example of this debate see "Two Viewpoints: Are Advanced Weapons Worth the Cost?," *Signal*, January 1987, pp. 29ff, which gives opposing opinions from Edward J. Walsh and Denny Smith. Many of the issues are reviewed by Walter Kross, *Military Reform: The High-Tech Debate in the Tactical Air Forces* (Washington: Government Printing Office, 1985).

how to deal with this problem. Critics believe that the military forces should rely on simpler and less sophisticated weapons in place of excessively complex systems now being developed. They argue that simpler systems will work better, and can be acquired in greater numbers because they cost less to purchase and operate. In their view, advanced technologies should be used only when they can be the basis for simple systems that are inexpensive, reliable, and easy to operate.[2]

There is no doubt but that the increasing use of advanced technologies can make it more difficult to build systems that are easy to use, reliable, and maintainable. Digital electronic systems are extremely problematic in this respect. Built-in test equipment (BITE), intended to automatically diagnose equipment malfunctions, often has been unreliable and inaccurate.[3] There is no intrinsic reason to believe that BITE diagnostic systems cannot

---

[2] This point was argued most notably by Franklin Spinney, *Defense Facts of Life: The Plans/Reality Mismatch* (Boulder: Westview Press, 1985). David R. Griffith, "High Technology Cited in Readiness Gap," *Aviation Week & Space Technology*, February 9, 1981, pp. 31-33, provided a short summary of Spinney's arguments when they first received public notice.

[3] If built-in test equipment works properly, it can automatically detect problems in electronic systems, making it possible for maintenance personnel to easily, quickly, and accurately isolate equipment failures. Unfortunately, they can mistakenly warn of faults that prove to be nonexistent and sometimes miss the problems that they were supposed to detect. Edward H. Kolcum, "Industry, Defense Dept. Focus Attention on Testing," *Aviation Week & Space Technology*, November 23, 1984, p. 76, notes that "False removal rates sometimes reach epidemic proportions.... In one study, 85% of suspected failures in the Boeing E-3C were found to be false."

be made to work. Although critics point to military failures in this area, the increasing use of automated test equipment in civilian applications suggests that it is an economically and commercially viable technology. This is also suggested by the experience of the U.S. military in developing automated test equipment, where experience has often led to improvements in the quality of BITE systems – a pattern also typical of the civilian sector which, in many cases, is adopting military initiatives.[4]

Supporters of advanced technology weapons, even those who may agree that sophisticated systems have often been unreliable and unmaintainable, argue that such problems are not inherent in the technology.[5] They contend that the difficulties arise mainly from the failure of equipment designers to give sufficient attention to building systems that are easy to operate, simple to maintain, and reliable. They believe that by changing design priorities it will be possible to develop sophisticated weapons that are reliable, maintainable, and usable. The real issue, they contend, is the need for better management.[6]

There is an element of truth in both positions. Weapons which are poorly designed, badly made,

---

[4] A U.S. Department of Defense program to build self-testing integrated circuits has been so successful that it is being copied by civilian firms. Larry Waller, "VHSIC Finally Builds A Head of Steam," *Electronics*, April 16, 1987, p. 84.

[5] "Too much, too soon: information overload," *Spectrum*, June 1987, pp. 51-55, provides examples of how equipment effectiveness can be radically altered by design changes.

[6] See Eric J. Lerner, "Reliability: the Air Force strikes back," *Aerospace America*, July 1986, pp. 16-18, and Edgar Ulsamer, "Down-to-Earth Concerns About Tactical Air," *Air Force Magazine*, April 1985, pp. 62-64.

difficult to maintain, and hard to operate have always existed, and cannot be attributed simply to the increased use of advanced technologies. If badly designed or built, even simple weapons can be unreliable and ineffective. The U.S. Army's LAW hand-held antitank rocket acquired such a reputation, although it was inexpensive and simple to use. This led the Israeli military to replace its LAWs with captured Soviet-made RPG-7 antitank grenade launchers. Similarly, the U.S. Army's TOW antitank missile is easier to use than the simpler, less costly Soviet AT-3 Sagger antitank missile. The Sagger missile is manually guided by its operator using a joy-stick, whereas the TOW has a command line-of-sight guidance that requires only that the operator keep the target on the cross-hairs of the sight. As a result, TOW operators can be trained more quickly and easily, and they can maintain proficiency in the use of the system with less effort.

Finally, it must be conceded that some extremely complex and hard to maintain military systems have proved to be highly effective. This was certainly true of the first generation of radars during the Second World War. They had a revolutionary impact on air and naval warfare despite their unreliability, cost, and mediocre man-machine interfaces. More recently, the American F-4E Phantom II fighter has been highly successful, even though it is considered to be one of the most complex fighter aircraft ever built.

The American M-1 battle tank is a system that provides some support for both points of view. Tests indicate that tank crews using the M-1 are considerably more effective than those using the older M-60. Although the new equipment is far more complicated, it is also easier to use and more capable, and even poor quality personnel can use it to obtain excellent results. Indeed, tests indicate an M-1 tank crew consisting of men of below average quality can kill more targets than an M-60 tank crew consisting of men of above average quality. At the same time, however, these advantages have been offset to some degree by the fact that some of the equipment on the tank is unreliable and difficult to maintain, posing serious problems for U.S. Army units in the field.[7]

The Management of High Technology

These sometimes contradictory examples tend to suggest that the problem with high technology systems is not inherent. More significant than problems with the technology are the design and management failures which fail to properly address the need to make a weapon reliable, repairable, and usable, and which fail to take into account possible trade-offs between such factors and performance. Thus, the human interaction with technology and the social organization of the exploitation of technology may prove critical in assessments of the usability of the new technologies.

Clearly, the successful exploitation of complex new technologies will not be easy, and the risks of failure will be high. The risks will grow as military forces become increasingly reliant on highly sophisticated systems. Although it will be possible to acquire new generation military systems that are usable, maintainable and affordable, it is also likely that much of the equipment will be expensive, and some of it will be hard to use and difficult to maintain. This suggests that the greatest challenges asso-

---

[7] These results are reported in Martin Binkin, *Military Technology and Defense Manpower* (Washington, D.C.: The Brookings Institution, 1986), pp. 54-55, 63-64.

ciated with the use of high technology may be managerial. As Seymour Deitchman has argued,

> while it is quite possible to go wrong by pressing technology too hard, it is also possible to make great gains in cost and capability by advancing to new generations of technology. It is no exaggeration to suggest that a technological revolution that is half digested may be far worse than one pursued without surcease. The problem is not with advanced technology but with unwise management of technological advance.[8]

Hence, considerable management skill will be needed to ensure that technologies are being most effectively exploited. To ensure that new systems work as expected, it will be necessary to make the trade-offs between performance on the one hand and reliability, maintainability, and operability on the other. Although it is sometimes possible to build high performance equipment that is also easy to use, often it is necessary to accept that devices will be less reliable, harder to maintain, and not as easy to employ. An M-60A3 is considerably more complex than the original M-60, because of the vastly increased use of electronic systems, and it is probably harder to keep the newer tank in fighting trim than the older one. Nevertheless, in this instance the increased performance justified the greater complexity. In contrast, the same justification could not be applied to the XM-803, even though it too had performance superior to that of the original M-60, since the complexity of the XM-803 was so great that its availability in combat situations was doubtful. To ensure that the new systems do not overwhelm

---

[8] *Military Power and the Advance of Technology*, p. 240.

available manpower resources, it will be necessary to conduct intensive training programs, ensure that systems can be operated by the men expected to use them, and to search for opportunities to reduce manning requirements.

The Israeli Experience

Israel's experience with sophisticated military systems during the past decade tends to support the views of those who believe that it is possible to make highly effective use of advanced technology. Many of Israel's highly complex weapons have performed well in combat. During the 1982 Lebanon War, F-15 and F-16 fighters, E-2C early warning aircraft, mini-RPVs, attack helicopters, reactive armor and electronic countermeasures all worked well. Indeed, the Israeli military has found that it is often possible to obtain major benefits by replacing simple, reliable, and effective systems with more expensive, more sophisticated, and more effective alternatives.[9]

Typical of the this approach has been the modernization of IDF's tank force. During the 1980s the Israeli Armored Corps upgraded many of its older tanks by providing them with laser rangefinders, digital fire control systems, reactive armor, and sophisticated night-vision equipment. Some of their newer tanks were given wind sensors and devices to measure barrel distortion as well. Such devices were adopted, despite their high cost and complexity, even though the simpler and

---

[9] W. Seth Carus, "Military Lessons of the 1982 Israel-Syria Conflict," pp. 261-280, in Robert Harkavy and Stephanie Neuman, eds., *The Lessons of Recent Wars in the Third World* (Lexington, Mass.: Lexington Books, 1985).

cheaper systems previously used had worked quite well. The IDF felt this equipment enabled tank crews to hit targets at longer ranges, and to engage targets more quickly. These capabilities are extremely important in battle, possibly decisive. During the fighting in Lebanon in 1982, Israeli Merkava tanks equipped with such gear destroyed Syrian tanks at ranges of up to 4,000 meters, using only a few shots to obtain each kill. Such remarkable achievements would have been impossible in the past.[10]

In general, the Israeli military has found that it is possible to develop extremely sophisticated weapons that ordinary soldiers find relatively easy to operate. The Israelis believe that there is no reason for advanced weapons to be either unreliable or ineffective. Israeli military engineers strongly believe that built-in test equipment and machine diagnostics can work if implemented properly. Weapons designers in Israel traditionally have paid attention to the needs of the men actually using the equipment, and they themselves often have considerable experience in the use of particular kinds of systems. Also, because of the close interrelationships between the military and the defense industrial infrastructure, equipment designers remain in close touch with users.[11]

---

[10] Carus, "Military Lessons of the 1982 Israel-Syria Conflict," pp. 270-273.

[11] Some of these issues were discussed in W. Seth Carus, *U.S. Procurement of Israeli Defense Goods and Services* (Washington, D.C.: American Israel Public Affairs Committee, 1984), pp. 10-13.

Infrastructure Considerations

Modern military forces have become dependent on a technical infrastructure, consisting of scientists, engineers, and technicians, laboratories, maintenance depots, and manufacturing facilities. This infrastructure acts as a force multiplier, providing technical support to ensure that weapons are used to maximum effectiveness, to modify existing equipment to enhance its effectiveness, to devise countermeasures to defeat enemy systems, or to develop equipment needed to meet a specific need that cannot be fulfilled with existing systems.

Examination of infrastructure considerations suggests that:

- Technical support is essential to the effective use of high technology military systems.

- Military forces relying on advanced weaponry require quick reaction capabilities to modify existing systems or to develop new ones in response to urgent operational requirements.

- The rapid pace of weapons innovation requires that existing systems be constantly upgraded to enhance existing capabilities, to provide new capabilities, or to provide countermeasures against new threats.

- It is no longer enough to deal with hardware: computer software is becoming increasingly important, often more so than the hardware it operates, and an ability to write and modify software is now essential.

Technical Support: Technically-qualified people can provide essential advice on the acquisition and utilization of equipment, a vital resource given the complexity of modern weapons. They can design and manufacture equipment domestically, which is often the only way of making sure that the devices meet local requirements and are available when needed. This is especially important if a quick reaction capability is required, since foreign arms manufacturers are unlikely to be able to produce new equipment with the same sense of urgency as locals with a serious stake in the outcome of the endeavor. Even if equipment is not designed and manufactured locally, but is obtained from other countries, local experts can ensure that the hardware meets local requirements and is not merely what the supplier is interested in peddling. They also can provide scientific intelligence, since they are able to identify unexpected threats and examine captured equipment.

A failure to exploit technology effectively can nullify the efforts of the most brilliant of scientists and engineers and the bravest of fighting men. Technology can be used to accomplish a great deal, but if misused it also can create substal problems. For example, during the Second World War the British fitted many of their bombers with tail warning radars to alert crews of the approach of German fighters. But, the Germans fitted their fighters with receivers that could detect the signals from the bomber radars, making it easy for them to locate and identify the British planes. The misapplied use of technology can be deadly.

During the 1982 Falklands War Argentinian bombs often failed to explode after hitting British ships – an example of how a lack of scientific and technical expertise can affect the conduct of military operations. Unable to penetrate British naval air-defenses at medium or high altitudes, the Argentinian pilots flew their aircraft at extremely low altitudes, often only a few feet above the water. This enabled them to reach Royal Navy ships unscathed, but also made their bombs ineffective. To ensure that a bomb does not destroy the aircraft that dropped it, bomb fuses become effective only after the bomb has traveled a certain distance. Because the Argentine aircraft were flying so low, in many cases the bombs did not go far enough. Even when the fuses did activate, they were set so that the bombs would explode only after a set period of time elapsed, to ensure that friendly aircraft had enough time to pass over the target. This meant that the bombs often passed completely through ships before finally detonating. In the final analysis, most, of the bombs that hit British ships never detonated.[12] Technically trained people could have anticipated the problem, and devised possible solutions. If the Argentinian military forces had possessed a comprehensive supporting technical infrastructure, the Falklands War could have ended differently.

The military significance of technical infrastructure was vividly demonstrated in many ways during the 1973 Arab-Israeli War. The Israeli Air Force, which had at its disposal the resources of Israel Aircraft Industries and its own internal maintenance and battle damage repair facilities, was able to quickly repair and return to service many damaged aircraft. In contrast, the Syrian and Egyptian Air Forces were unable to do so. As a result, relatively few aircraft were available for service when the fighting came to an end.[13] Israeli experts also made it possible to rapidly employ the new types of equipment provided by the United States in an

---

[12] Jeffrey Ethell and Alfred Price, *Air War South Atlantic* (New York: Macmillan Publishing Company, 1983), pp. 64-65, discuss the problem. On p. 183 they estimate that 75% of Argentinian bombs failed to detonate.

[13] Jasjit Singh, *Air Power in Modern Warfare* (New Delhi, India: Lacer International, 1985), pp. 100-101.

emergency airlift.

Quick Reaction Capabilities: Modern military forces must be able to rapidly develop and field new types of equipment, either by modifying existing systems or through the development of wholly new devices. This need can result from the unexpected appearance of enemy systems with new capabilities or from the failure of friendly systems to work as anticipated. In either case, it often will be necessary to quickly provide friendly forces with new devices or with new versions of old equipment.

Acquiring such quick reaction capabilities is not easy. It is necessary to disregard established bureaucratic procedures to speed up decision-making. Bureaucracies often resist change, even under the pressures of a war and red tape can continue even as the battle progresses. Specific kinds of technical capabilities are also required. Intelligence agencies and field forces must be able to identify problem areas, often based on partial information obtained from an analysis of ongoing military operations. Following this, technical agencies must discover possible solutions to the problems that can be fielded as quickly as possible. Thus, the entire development cycle, from the identification of equipment requirements, through design and development, testing, to the final production, must be reduced from a period that normally can take months or years into a few hours, days, or weeks. This can only happen if a military force can call on high quality people (working in equally good facilities) who are willing to work long hours, perhaps beyond the limits of their endurance.

The 1982 Falklands War provides a number of good examples that illustrate the importance of quick reaction capabilities. The British military had not anticipated fighting a war in the South Atlantic, and it quickly discovered that much of its equipment was ill-suited for such a conflict and that it did not have systems needed to perform certain essential missions. In many cases, it proved possible for the British to field equipment that met immediate requirements. Among the most important projects was the modification of Royal Air Force Harriers so that they could operate from aircraft carriers, thus increasing the number of fighters available to the Royal Navy task force. These Harriers were also given an air-to-air combat capability, which they previously had lacked, as well as new electronic warfare systems. It took only about 15 days to make "Blue Eric" jamming pods for the Harriers. In addition, the antiship-missile defenses of the aircraft carriers were quickly enhanced by taking an existing jamming system, modifying it to work against Exocet antiship missiles, and fitting it into helicopters stationed on the ships.

Israel has developed impressive capabilities of a similar nature, as was demonstrated during the 1973 war. The Israeli military was able to devise and employ a large number of field expedients needed to deal with unexpected situations. This was especially important in the area of electronic warfare, where considerable work was done during the fighting to provide Israeli aircraft with enhanced protection against Arab surface-to-air missiles. In addition, it was easier to react to unexpected threats, since the technical expertise needed to analyze the problem was close at hand. Long lines of communication were avoided, and the experts could be brought into direct contact with the people actually doing the fighting.

Weapons Upgrades: Modernization programs to enhance the battlefield performance, reliability, maintainability, or survivability of existing weapons systems have become essential, since the constant pace of technical innovation makes all weapons potentially obsolete or obsolescent in relatively short periods of time. Since ships, aircraft, and tanks can have a life span of 30 years, or even more (some U.S. Navy aircraft carriers will remain in service for up to 50 years), weapons systems will have to be upgraded several times during their operational life. When the rapid rate at which technology is improving is coupled with the time it takes to develop and field new equipment, it not surprising that some platforms carry equipment that is already out-of-date even as they enter service. Because of the rapidity with which equipment can become obsolete modern platforms must be designed so that they can be upgraded with relative ease.

In this context, obsolescence has several meanings. In some cases, it means only that equipment with greater capabilities has appeared, but nevertheless the existing equipment remains serviceable. The low-light night-vision equipment adopted in the late 1970s, which enhanced existing light, remains useful, despite the advent of newer infrared imaging systems. Not only do the infrared systems provide better images at night, but they are also useful when visibility is reduced during daytime. In such instances, the decision to upgrade depends on cost and performance: the new systems ought to be adopted if the improvement in capability is great enough and if the cost is low enough.[14]

---

[14] Other considerations also come into play. Reliability and maintainability are important. It often makes sense to replace electronic systems merely because newer devices are easier to repair or break down less often. Similarly, newer electronic systems are often smaller, produce less heat, and consume less electricity, all additional benefits.

In other cases, equipment inadequacies can seriously affect performance in battle. This is especially true in the area of electronic warfare. Ships, aircraft, and armored vehicles rely on electronic warfare systems to survive on the battlefield, and these systems often have to be enhanced to deal with new types of threats. Thus, the introduction of laser-guided missiles has made it necessary to provide helicopters with laser-warning devices. Similarly, the emergence of laser-guided antitank weapons has led many countries to provide their tanks with sensors to detect laser beams, and smoke countermeasures to block the beams.[15] In the future, it is likely that tanks will be provided with radar warning receivers and electronic countermeasures to defend against the new generation of weapons using millimeter wave radars. Failure to provide countermeasures may make it impossible for platforms to survive.

Upgrading need not be expensive. The reactive armor that the Israelis added to their old main battle tanks before the 1982 Lebanon War to protect them against antitank missiles required an investment of only about $10,000 per tank – a minuscule amount compared with the $2 million or more required to buy a new tank. Similarly, they were able to significantly enhance the effectiveness of their tanks by the use of improved antitank rounds that cost about the same as the older ammunition.[16]

All upgrade programs will not be so cheap, but

---

[15] C.I. Coleman, "Laser threat warning: a growing need on the battlefield," *International Defense Review*, July 1986, pp. 965-967.

[16] Carus, "Military Lessons of the 1982 Israel-Syria Conflict," pp. 270-272.

enemy radars, and gave them an improved rocket fuel, a better warhead, and an enhanced seeker. Similarly, early model TOW antitank missiles were given larger warheads and a more powerful rocket motor so that they could penetrate the better-protected new-generation tanks.

Arab countries also have acquired an ability to modify existing equipment. Egypt, Jordan, and Syria all have tank upgrade programs. Both Egypt and Syria are taking old Soviet tanks and providing them with better ammunition, improved fire control systems, and (in the case of Egypt) new guns. The Jordanians are modifying their old British-built Centurion tanks to make them comparable to new American-supplied tanks. The ability of Arab countries to enhance their equipment is likely to grow in the future.

Computer Software: New military systems are heavily dependent on integrated digital computers. Critical to their performance is the quality of the software. Systems like the AWACS, which may have a million or more lines of computer code, are now the norm, not the exception.

Through the 1970s, the main constraints on computer systems were the size, cost, reliability, and power of the hardware. This is no longer the case. It is now possible to acquire computers able to survive in military environments that are also extremely powerful, take up little space, have a high degree of reliability, and are relatively inexpensive. Computer software is now the main constraint. It now can be more expensive to write the software than it is to buy the hardware, and the least reliable part of the system may be the software. The Commander of the U.S. Air Force's Electronic Combat Directorate has noted that from a technical point of view, "the biggest hurdle we have right now is the software."[20]

Fortunately, the growing power of the hardware has made it easier to produce software that is "user friendly" and that performs more and more quickly. Unfortunately, the high cost of writing and maintaining military software has meant that many existing programs are now out of date and do not conform to current human engineering standards.

The central role of software has significant implications for the operational effectiveness. It may be the software that makes a system more or less advanced, and not the hardware. Thus, when the United States sold Pakistan AN/ALR-69 electronic warfare pods, the hardware was identical to the U.S. Air Force pods but because the software was not the same the Pakistani pods had inferior performance.[21] It also means that equipment upgrades may take the form of loading new programs, not of modifying the hardware, further complicating efforts to compare opposing military forces.

The growing importance of software has important infrastructure implications. First, it will be necessary to modify software during fighting to adapt to changing circumstances. In the 1982 Falklands War, Britain's navy discovered some serious flaws in the software for their Sea Wolf shipboard anti-aircraft missiles. To correct the problems, programmers in Britain wrote new code and then the revised software was transmitted by

---

[20] Interview with Brig. Gen. Noah Loy as printed in *Defense News*, November 23, 1987, p. 38.

[21] *Aviation Week & Space Technology*, December 6, 1982, p. 19, and *Defense Electronics*, February 1983, p. 11.

satellite to the ships in the South Atlantic.[22]

Incidents of this type are likely to become increasingly common. Military forces will need to have capabilities to update and modify the programs that control high-tech weaponry. Most countries with advanced weapons industries will eventually learn to write their own software, but it will take time for this to happen.

The growing importance of software also has some arms trade implications. The United States naturally wants to protect the programs of its military equipment, because they provide much of its advantage over potential adversaries. This can create problems for friendly governments, as the United States distributes its software in a form that ensures that users cannot read it or modify it. Although this is justifiable, it makes it virtually impossible for friendly countries to quickly modify the code to meet unexpected problems. This is one important explanation for the strong desire of countries like Israel and Singapore to obtain access to source code. Eventually the United States may have to work out procedures that will protect American security interests and yet meet legitimate requirements of allies.

In the Arab-Israeli military balance, Arab countries will have difficulty competing with Israel in the production of custom software to operate new systems. Although an increasing amount of software is now written in Arab countries, it generally involves maintenance of software originally written in

---

[22] This feat is noted in passing in "Air Defense Missiles Limited Tactics of Argentine Aircraft," *Aviation Week & Space Technology*, July 19, 1982, p. 22, and in the British White Paper on the Falklands War, *The Falklands Campaign: The Lessons* (London: Her Majesty's Stationary Office, 1982), p. 21.

the United States or Western Europe, and no Arab country has sophisticated software engineering capabilities.[23]

In contrast, Israel has world-class computer scientists, some of whom are now involved in the development of sophisticated artificial intelligence, command and control, and signal-processing systems. This was demonstrated in many of the programs associated with the Lavi fighter, such as the SPS (self-protection systems) electronic warfare suite or the weapons control systems. Not only does this make it possible for Israel to develop specialty software to meet its own unique needs at lower cost than acquiring it from the United States, but it permits constant adjustment to meet changing requirements.

The Role of the Scientific-Technical Infrastructure

When evaluating a country's military power it may be as important to examine the scientific and technical infrastructure as it is to examine equipment inventories and order of battle. This infrastructure can enhance the effectiveness of military forces and reduce vulnerability to opposing systems. Conversely, the absence of such support may make it impossible to effectively exploit high technology.

There is reason to believe that Israel will be a

---

[23] For example, the maintenance software for Jordan's F-1 fighters was written in France. See "F1s at Azraq Take Interceptor/Ground Attack Role," *Aviation Week & Space Technology*, June 27, 1983, p. 75. On the other hand, Jordan will have the ability to maintain the software written in the United States for its new automated air defense system, according to *Middle East Economic Digest*, October 31, 1987, p. 42.

major victor in the competition to exploit advanced technology weapons. Despite the growing size and sophistication of Arab arms industries, Israel's defense infrastructure is considerably more capable and the gap is especially great where high technology is concerned. In many areas, Israel is able to produce equipment equal in sophistication to that made in the United States and Western Europe, and is sometimes able to make innovative systems available nowhere else.

In contrast, Arab countries will remain dependent on foreign sources through at least the mid-1990s. They will not have the research and development facilities required to design new equipment. Although they will be capable of exploiting increasingly sophisticated technologies, they have a long way to go before reaching even the level of the more advanced Third World arms producers, like Brazil.

This dependence on foreign expertise severely limits the potential contribution that Arab arms industries can make to the performance of Arab military forces. If a new problem emerges, they must go to a foreign supplier for a solution. In wartime this will work only if the supplying country has an off-the-shelf system, because the development of new equipment (or of modifications to existing equipment) will take a considerable amount of time. It does not allow quick reaction capabilities or the development of surprise weapons.

Significantly, Egypt, which has the most capable Arab arms industry, also is the only Arab country to have made peace with Israel, while Syria, which is the leader of the rejectionist front, has one of the least capable. Israel's edge over the Syrians is particularly sizable. Syria has only a limited technical infrastructure, and is heavily dependent on Soviet equipment and expertise. The types of equipment that the

Syrians will need to obtain, especially countermeasures, will be extremely difficult to obtain. The Soviets will be reluctant to supply their own devices, even if they have appropriate ones. Thus, the Syrians will find it especially difficult to compete in this high technology battlefield.

Nevertheless, most Arab countries can modify equipment to some extent. This is reflected in the proliferation of tank upgrade programs. Egypt, Jordan, and Syria have mounted such efforts, and in some cases the results are quite impressive. Although the programs are heavily dependent on foreign components, they presage an era in which Arab military forces will be able to rely on indigenous weapons modifications to enhance systems performance.

7: The Human Context of the New Technologies

Even in the most technological of battlefield environments, replete with autonomous and semi-autonomous machines, the skills, bravery, ingenuity, and intelligence of the people using and directing the use of the equipment will remain critical. Although machines may make it possible for men to accomplish otherwise impossible tasks, human intelligence is required to ensure that the equipment is used in the most effective ways and that it is operating according to expectation.

The Human Context of Military Operations

The human context manifests itself at various levels -- national strategic decision-making, operational and tactical military planning, and the individual combatant. In all cases, human actions can have a decisive impact on the conduct of military operations, even when these are largely dependent on highly sophisticated systems.

Military strategy involves the conscious integration of military capabilities, including the operational characteristics of weapons, with national objectives. Although often ignored in technical studies of war, the importance of the political and strategic factors is so great that it can overwhelm the military-technical issues. The mere possession of equipment does not ensure that it is going to be used effectively, or that it is going to achieve meaningful results. What is required is conscious effort to understand both rationale for the use of military forces, and the capabilities of those forces.

The history of the Israel Air Force provides an example of how the development of military forces can be guided by broader policy considerations. Israeli air power, which has dominated the Arab-Israeli military balance for twenty years, did not develop by accident, but rather is the result of deliberate decisions. Before the 1967 war, defense officials decided that it made sense to rely heavily on air power and so diverted to the air force resources that could easily have been used for other purposes. They recognized that a powerful air force could defend strategic targets from air attack, support standing army units defending borders in the event of an unexpected enemy attack and at the same time protect the mobilization of reserve units, and provide a powerful offensive force as well. Equally important, reliance on air power enabled Israel to maximize the benefits of its highly educated but small population. The air force required only relatively small numbers of people to produce considerable combat power.

For national strategy, weapons and other military systems are only tools. The capabilities of military hardware define the limits of what is and is not possible in military operations.

The planning of military operations and tactics

also depends heavily on the skills of the people involved in the process. Decisions to employ or not employ military forces in particular ways can have a decisive impact on the effectiveness of those forces. Some of these issues are discussed in more detail in the next chapter, where the importance of tactics and operational methods are examined.

Egyptian military planning in the years prior to the 1973 war provides a good example of how careful military planning can overcome weaknesses in equipment. The Egyptians recognized that Israel had superior air and armored forces, and that to win a war they had to somehow find a way of neutralizing these advantages.

The solution of the Egyptian General Staff was to strengthen defenses against Israeli aircraft and tanks, and to adopt operational methods that reduced the risks and that emphasized their strengths. They invested enormous resources in a massive air-defense network that included 450 radars, 150 surface-to-air missile batteries, thousands of SA-7 hand-held missiles, large numbers of anti-aircraft guns, and hundreds of fighter aircraft. They also built-up the defenses of their ground forces, providing them with more tanks and a comprehensive array of antitank weapons: mines, RPG-7 grenade launchers, Sagger missiles, guns of various sizes, including SU-100 self-propelled guns.

To make these forces effective, the Egyptians adopted a carefully prepared operational plan. The ground forces that crossed to the east, Israeli-held side of the Suez Canal were to remain within range of the air defenses located on the west side of the canal, so that they would not be vulnerable to Israeli air attacks. They also were to remain on the tactical defensive once they secured their positions on the Is-raeli side of the canal -- forcing Israeli armored forces to mount costly attacks against powerful antitank defenses.[1]

This example illustrates the extent to which careful military planning can compensate for technical weaknesses, like the inferiority of much of Egypt's military equipment to Israel's. The inferior performance of their tanks mattered less when the conflict was transformed from a tank-on-tank battle to one in which Israeli tanks were faced by a complex of antitank weapons (of which tanks formed only a small part). Similarly, Egyptian inferiority in the air was less important when they could rely on ground-based air defenses.

At the level of the individual combatant, the effectiveness of a tank or aircraft depends on the willingness of the men operating the equipment to take risks, and on their skill in utilizing the capabilities of the machinery. Important in this respect are motivation and sense of responsibility. Even simple equipment will be useless if soldiers are unwilling to learn how to use it effectively, or if they do not use it with courage and aggressiveness.

Naval warfare provides some interesting examples of how crews determine effectiveness of warships, despite dependence on machines of all kinds. The survivability of a warship clearly depends on its ability to avoid being hit by enemy weapons, and on its built-in resistance to damage. But the ability of crews to repair damage and to control its impact is just as important. This was vividly demonstrated by the successful efforts of the crew of

---

[1] The plan fell apart only when pressure from the Syrians forced the Egyptians to abandon their defensive posture for an offensive one. The Egyptians left the protected area, and their ground forces suffered heavy losses. This opened the way for the successful Israeli counterattack across the canal that ultimately led to the encirclement of the Third Army.

the U.S. Navy frigate Stark to save their ship after being hit by two Iraqi Exocet antiship missiles in May 1987. If the crew had been less well trained in the techniques of damage control, it is possible that the Stark may not have survived.

Courage and skill cannot always compensate for inferior weaponry, and the bravest and most skilled fighting men will fail if fighting adversaries with weapons that give them superiority in battle. The Israelis discovered this in the opening stages of the 1973 war, when their aircraft were exposed to SA-6 missiles and their tanks to Sagger missiles. Yet, even in this case, the success of the weapons depended on the skill and bravery of the Egyptian and Syrian soldiers who operated them, and on the tactical and operational skill with which they were employed. Moreover, these weapons became available to soldiers only because of the people who had the foresight to acquire them.

It is dangerous to focus excessively on the hardware of war without taking into account the character and skills of the people who direct and operate military forces. Although weapons can be decisive, there are limits to the extent to which even the best designed machines can compensate for human error – and they certainly cannot correct mistaken military strategies or operational methods.

The Human Context and Air Warfare – An Example

Air warfare is probably that form of warfare most dependent on technology, yet success in it remains dependent on the human factor. Despite the sophisticated systems now employed in air combat, the skills of fighter pilots are still critical to the outcome. British analysts believe that the success of their fighters during the 1982 Falklands War can be attributed in large measure to the greater combat skills of the Royal Navy pilots.[2] Similarly, it is generally believed that the superiority of the Israel Air Force over its Arab adversaries lies in the skill of its pilots. An Israeli F-15 is more capable than a Saudi F-15, because of the greater skills and experience of the Israeli pilots.

Similarly, the effectiveness of ground attack operations can depend in large measure on the skills and bravery of pilots. This was clearly demonstrated by the performance of Argentinian pilots during the 1982 Falklands War, when they often flew only a few feet off the water into dense air defenses to drop bombs on British warships.

But skills of pilots cannot completely compensate for fundamental inequalities in weaponry. In a confrontation between two pilots of equal skill, the one flying the most capable plane will have the edge. An aircraft equipped with an all-aspect air-to-air missile, like the Sidewinder AIM-9L, has an advantage over a plane with an older generation missile and a smaller engagement envelope.

As will be discussed in detail in the next chapter, the battlefield has become more integrated and pilots are increasingly a part of an intricate web that support their operations. Thus, an Israeli pilot flying over the Bekaa Valley during the 1982 Lebanon War was supported by maintenance crews at his air base, by radar operators in E-2C airborne early warning aircraft and at ground command stations, by elec-

---

[2] Alfred Price, "The Falklands Conflict: A New Look at The Lessons for Air Warfare," pp. 11-14 in Charles H. Wiseman, ed., *The International Countermeasures Handbook 1986*, 11th Edition (Palo Alto, Ca.: EW Communications, 1986), notes the vital importance of such factors during the 1982 Falklands War.

tronic warfare specialists operating in aircraft and on the ground, by communications personnel who made possible the transmission of information from one system to another, and by planning and intelligence officers who gathered and analyzed information about enemy targets and threats and who planned the operations. Although physically alone, the pilot was in fact part of a human system that required the coordinated and effective participation of thousands of people.

The extent to which the context can make a difference is suggested by the impact of turn-around time and sortie generation.[3] Well-trained maintenance teams, used effectively, can have a substantial impact on the extent to which aircraft can be kept in service. Even though two air forces may operate identical aircraft, the number of sorties that can be generated per plane can vary a great deal. According to one estimate, the Israel Air Force can generate a maximum of 4.5 sorties per day per aircraft, compared with only 3.0 sorties for Jordan, and 2.0 for Syria. During sustained operations, this source suggests that Israel could still generate 2.5 sorties per plane per day, and Syria only 1.0.[4] If these calculations are correct, the IAF can fly more than twice as many operations as the Syrian Air Force, even though the two forces operate the same number of aircraft.

---

[3] Although these comments concentrate on the extent to which maintenance can affect the pace of operations, there is also a materiel side to this equation, as suggested in the previous chapter, since it is possible to build equipment that is more reliable and easier to repair.

[4] Kenneth S. Brower, "The Middle East military balance: Israel versus the rest," *International Defense Review*, July 1987, p. 907.

Manpower Quality and High Technology Weapons

A decade ago it was widely believed that new technologies would make it possible to operate equipment with poorer quality manpower. Especially in the United States, it was hoped that with the end of the draft it would be possible to use people with less training and education and with lower intelligence scores to man highly sophisticated equipment by making the new devices easier to operate and maintain. Line replaceable units and automated test equipment were expected to reduce the amount of time required to detect and isolate equipment malfunctions, and to make it easier to replace the faulty devices.[5]

Many of these expectations have not come to pass. Maintenance support equipment proved to require more skills to operate than anticipated, and the people assigned to do maintenance work lacked the skills needed to deal with unexpected problems. As a result, many of the weapons that entered service in the 1970s and early 1980s suffered from poor reliability and often proved difficult to maintain.

In retrospect, it is evident that the quality of manpower required has not declined. If anything the skills needed have increased, even if some weapons become easier to use and maintain. Experience suggests that while automatic systems can handle many routine tasks, when problems do emerge it is necessary to have highly trained and intelligent people at hand to analyze and resolve them. Although under many circumstances it might be possible to reduce training, as a general rule the

---

5 The discussion that follows draws heavily on Martin Binkin, *Military Technology and Defense Manpower* (Washington, D.C.: The Brookings Institution, 1986).

skills required are going to increase, as will the need for training.

In many cases, the tasks that ordinary soldiers are being asked to perform now involve a degree of decision which previously would have been made by a superior. Thus, a missile gunner armed with a Stinger anti-aircraft missile has the potential fighting power of a whole battery of anti-aircraft guns. In the past, the responsibility of commanding the anti-aircraft battery would have belonged to an experienced officer. Today, a missile team might be commanded by a noncommissioned officer of limited experience. To expect a relatively inexperienced and possibly poorly trained soldier of low rank to decide in a few seconds whether or not he should fire his missile at a particular target is asking for trouble.

Many of the problems associated with the use of high technology weapons will result from the increasing extent to which low ranking soldiers will be required to handle conceptual issues requiring command decisions. Although it is possible for junior people to make such decisions, they can only perform effectively if properly selected and trained. Thus, even in cases where equipment may be easy to operate, using it in battle may be more difficult because of the complexity of the decisions that have to be made by the users.

Finally, there are dangers in relying on men to use technology that they do not understand. Poor-quality or inexperienced soldiers abuse and misuse equipment, and they do not take maximum advantage of its capabilities. Use of technology can create vulnerabilities, and a lack of awareness of such vulnerabilities can lead to catastrophic failures. This was vividly demonstrated during the 1982 Lebanon War, when the Israelis were able to exploit weaknesses in the Syrian command and control system to jam communications and (according to Soviet sources) to pass along false orders.

The requirement for high quality manpower will pose a severe problem for all military organizations, although those based on voluntary enlistment will face especially severe difficulties. The technical skills needed to maintain and operate advanced military systems are to a large extent the same as those required in the civilian sector. Hence, in many cases the military will lose trained personnel to civilian industries offering better pay and working conditions. This has traditionally been a problem for air forces, and it should become increasingly true for armies as well.

Syrian and Israeli Perspectives of the Human Context

It is generally agreed by both Syrians and Israelis that the human factor will remain critical in the outcome of battles in the Middle East, despite the increasing use of sophisticated military systems. Syria's Defense Minister, Mustafa Tlas, has stated that

> The October [1973] liberation war has proved that the human element is the most important factor [in a future battle with Israel]. We believe that victory depends primarily on preparing the fighters physically, mentally, and morally. Although modern weapons have a significant role to play, man remains the primary and most important element.[6]

---

[6] *Al-Majallah* (London), 11-17 December 1985, p. 11, in Arabic, as translated in FBIS, *Daily Report: Middle East and Africa*, December 12, 1985, p. H1.

Most Israelis would agree with this assessment. David Elazar, the Chief of Staff of the Israeli Defense Forces during the 1973 war, said that the quality of an army is depended on: "Primarily, the soldiers' will to fight, their motivation and readiness for sacrifice," and he continued:

> The qualitative level of an army is a direct function of the level of the people, their sense of national identity, and their cultural and technological sophistication.
>
> The quality of an army is a result of its efficiency, organization, training, specialization, discipline and the ability of its junior and senior officers to command.[7]

More recently, an Israeli analyst has suggested that the military power of a nation can be determined by:

> planning, decision-making, and organizational talent, as well as the more intangible qualities of command, and the combatant's personal proficiency, capacity for improvisation, and ability to withstand privation and stress.[8]

Thus, intangible leadership and organizational factors also can influence combat performance.

The critical starting point in the assessment of manpower quality is the motivation of soldiers — their willingness to serve in the military, to learn the

---

[7] David Elazar, "The Yom Kippur War: Military Lessons," in *Military Aspects of the Israeli-Arab Conflict* (Tel Aviv, Israel: University Publishing Project, 1975), p. 247.

[8] Zvi Lanir, "The Qualitative Factor in the Israeli-Arab Arms Race of the Late 1980s," *IDF Journal*, 3 (Fall 1985), p. 27.

skills required to perform their tasks, and to fight. Such things, however, are difficult to measure under the best of circumstances, and can vary considerably over time. Hence, it is difficult to make universally true blanket statements, except that no country in the Middle East has a monopoly on bravery or motivation. The only advantage Israel possesses in this respect is the widespread recognition by its soldiers that the survival of the country may depend on the successes of the military.

Differences become more evident when examining levels of education, and especially of technical training. Although standards of education and technical training in the Arab world have improved substantially in the past two decades, Israel still maintains a significant edge. In 1961, the literacy rate in Jordan was only 31 percent, but in 1987 the figure was up to 74 percent.[9] In Syria literacy rates doubled between 1960 and 1978, from 29.5 percent to 58 percent.[10] But only 56 percent of Syrian children of secondary school age attend such institutions, and only 16 percent attend a school beyond the secondary level.[11]

By comparison, 78 percent of Israeli children attend secondary schools, and 34 percent receive additional schooling. The number of people with a high level of technical expertise in the Israeli population has grown in recent years, reflected in

---

[9] According to the Jordanian Ministry of Education. *Middle East Economic Digest*, September 26, 1987, p. 28.

[10] World Bank, *World Tables*, 3rd Edition, Volume II (Baltimore: Johns Hopkins University Press, 1984), p. 87.

[11] World Bank, *World Development Report*, (New York: Oxford University Press, 1986).

the high-tech industrial base now in place. Free primary and secondary education, combined with the training given to new recruits, has made it possible for the Israeli military to keep pace with the growing sophistication of its equipment. To this end, the IDF maintains very close links with the education system. Israeli high schools, especially the technical high schools, work in close cooperation with the military, turning out technical support personnel who serve in all branches of the standing army. Many of these people will serve in the regular military into their early thirties. The universities also play an important role. Academic training is offered to those who sign on for additional stints of service. At some universities, such as the Technion in Haifa and the Weizman Institute in Rehovot, the inter-relationship between civilian and military research is extremely close. In some cases, the needs of the military research establishment can determine the courses taught or the curriculum offered.

On the whole, the average Israeli soldier enters the military with better education than his Arab counterpart, and receives better training once in uniform. The training of tank crews provides a telling example of the difference in the quality of manpower and the relative adaptability and ingenuity of soldiers in the region. An Israeli crew member is trained to do every major task associated with the operation of a tank: the driver can perform the tasks of the gunner, the gunner can replace the driver, and the loader can act as gunner. The crewman is also taught how to maintain his tank, and is expected to perform most routine maintenance tasks. This is usually not the case in Arab armies, although the Jordanians and, increasingly, the Egyptians are important exceptions. If one member of a Syrian tank crew is killed or wounded, the survivors cannot replace him since they have not been trained to do his tasks. As a result, the tank will be operated at far below performance or not at all. As tanks become more sophisticated and the crews require even more specialized training, this problem will be further exacerbated.

Despite this, Arab military forces have enough technically skilled manpower to accomplish most tasks, and are in a position to exploit systems requiring limited technical expertise the remaining personnel. In addition, most Arab military forces employ foreign advisors and technicians to operate and maintain sophisticated equipment, but their loyalties in time of war may be dubious. Countries that are particularly dependent on foreign manpower assistance include Syria, with several thousand Soviet advisors, and Saudi Arabia which relies on tens of thousands of American, European, Pakistani, and other foreign technicians and soldiers.

The major difference between Israel and the Arab world, however, rests in the area of scientific capability and advanced engineering. Israeli scientific and technical institutes and high-technology companies are extremely advanced. Israel has one of the highest ratios of scientists to population in the world, and in many areas it has world-class scientific and technical talent. This ensures that Israeli technical endeavors are often of considerable sophistication, comparable to those of Western Europe or the United States, as discussed in the previous chapter.

In contrast, the Arab world has few such resources. Progress has been made in the past two decades, but there is still a wide gap between Israel and its potential adversaries. Although it is true that an increasing number of Arab students are studying abroad, and that scientific and technical institutions are beginning to emerge, the current lack of local institutions that can work in conjunction with the military remains an impediment.

The training of the relatively few good people in the Arab forces has been rigid and not conducive to exercise of the ingenuity required during times of stress. Israeli soldiers, are better equipped to handle spontaneous crises, in part because they have been trained to do so. Given the high premium that is being placed on the ability to interfere with the operational aspects of systems in future conflict, this aspect of the human equation has taken on added importance.

Israel's Demographic Problem

Given the disparity between the size of Israel's forces and those of the Arabs,[12] and the sensitivity of Israel to casualties, Israel has strong incentives to use new technologies to reduce the number of people required to operate its military forces and to reduce the number of casualties that it is likely to sustain during a conflict. Military requirements are a heavy burden on Israeli society and individuals.

Creative exploitation of new technologies can significantly reduce the number of people required for operation or maintenance. Israel has been able to drastically reduce the number of people needed to maintain the equipment for its reserve combat units by relying on climate-controlled storage containers.

---

[12] According to Aharon Levran and Zeev Eytan, *The Middle East Military Balance 1986* (Boulder, Colorado: Westview Press, 1987), p. 398, Israel's standing military forces were only a third the size of Syria's (170,000 compared with 500,000).]

Such equipment also enhances battle readiness. A relatively small number of people can keep the equipment battle-ready, fully armed and fueled. Similarly, the Israel Air Force has been able to reduce its manpower by aggressively searching for methods of substituting machines for people or cutting the number of man-hours required to accomplish particular tasks.

Despite such successes, however, Israel may not be able to reduce its overall military manpower requirements through reliance on new technologies. Even with the availability of labor saving equipment, the new technologies are increasing the number of tasks that have to be performed. The number of people required to operate complex intelligence-gathering systems is growing, despite increasing automation, largely because the effectiveness of the new intelligence systems involve a whole host of new tasks that did not exist in the past. Similarly, electronic warfare systems that twenty years ago barely existed now account for a significant portion of the total military effort, and require a large number of high quality people.

Israel also may have problems producing the manpower needed. Training will become more important, and allocations of manpower between various parts of the military will have to be carefully weighed. The problems will be compounded by reliance on reservists who will have to be taken away from civilian jobs for tours of military service to be retrained on new systems.

To a certain extent, the reduction in the size of the Israel Air Force could be a major benefit to the other services. Many technically proficient people should become available to maintain the increasingly sophisticated systems going to the ground forces. This process may be accelerated by the increased use of equipment that is easier to maintain, when aircraft like the F-4E Phantoms are upgraded.

The Impact of the Human Context

Because of the critical importance of people in the successful exploitation of weapons, and because of the superior quality of Israeli manpower, on the whole the new technologies will tend to benefit Israel more than the Syrians.

To the extent that new weapons are easy to operate and maintain, the Syrians should benefit, since it will allow them to use low quality manpower to reduce the qualitative gap between their military forces and Israel's. The possibilities offered by powerful, inexpensive weapons were vividly demonstrated during the 1973 war. The Egyptian and Syrian armies were able to distribute large numbers of Soviet-supplied SA-7 hand-held anti-aircraft missiles and AT-3 Sagger antitank missiles to their infantry, providing protection against Israeli aircraft and armored forces. Without those weapons, the effectiveness of Arab ground forces would have decreased dramatically.

At the same time, to the extent that the new weapons are difficult to operate and maintain, Israel will be the main beneficiary because of its higher levels of technical skill. The gap remains quite large, despite the improving quality of Arab manpower, as is shown by the different experiences of the Israeli and Egyptian air forces in adopting the F-4E Phantom II fighter. The F-4E is a highly complex aircraft, difficult to operate and maintain because of its reliance on 1960s vintage technologies. Yet, the Israeli Air Force was able to make effective use of its F-4Es almost as soon as they were brought into service, requiring only limited American technical support even though less then a year had passed since the order to buy the aircraft was placed. In contrast, the Egyptian Air Force, which also had little time to prepare for the arrival of its F-4Es, for many years required the assistance of American technical teams, and the operational readiness of its Phantoms remains relatively low. This experience suggests that some Arab military forces may have difficulties dealing with the complexities of advanced technology weapons systems.

8: New Technologies and the Operational Art of War

It is too soon to predict the impact of the new generation of military systems on the manner in which wars will be fought. Many of the new technologies have not been tested in action, so one can only speculate on their true operational effectiveness. Even when equipment has been used in battle, the experience has often been too limited to allow more than a generalized understanding of its potential. Another limiting factor is the difficulty in fully understanding the interaction between new systems and the host of existing systems deployed on the battlefield. And this does not even take into account the interactions between the different, untried new systems whose operational characteristics are only partially understood. Moreover, the effectiveness of systems is ultimately dependent on the manner in which they are used, and it often requires some experience in battle before optimal techniques are developed.

Despite these problems, it is possible to make some general observations about the likely impact of the new technologies on warfare. In important respects, the future battlefield will be similar to what we have known in the past. Tactics and operational methods will remain important, as will the close-in battlefield, and the individual soldier. At the same time, however, the increased lethality of weapons, improvements in intelligence gathering, and the increased integration of military systems will change the character of the battlefield in fundamental ways. Adjustments in tactics and operational methods will have to be made to cope with the new circumstances, but the particular methods adopted will depend to a large extent on the specific matrix of weapons and tactics employed by the opposing forces. Countermeasures and surprise weapons will become increasingly important.

Five general observations appear particularly important in this respect.

- Tactics and operational methods will continue to be decisive on the battlefield, which means that the effectiveness of new weapons will depend in part on the ability of users to develop effective means of employing them.

- Military effectiveness will depend increasingly on the coordinated, integrated use of a variety of individual systems, emphasizing the importance of command and control systems, of battle management, and force integration.

- The close-in battle will remain critical despite the development of deep-strike systems.

- The potential lethality of individual weapons is increasing, but actual effectiveness in battle will depend on enemy countermeasures and on camouflage, concealment, and deception.

- Electronic warfare, including use of electronic countermeasures and counter-C^3 measures, will continue to grow in importance.

The Primacy of Tactics and Operational Methods

The enthusiasm for new military systems, and the desire for the quantum leaps in capability that they can provide, often lead people to ignore the central importance of tactics and operational methods. A highly capable weapon that is misused, or that is used out of context, may provide no more combat capability than a far less sophisticated system. Similarly, an older piece of equipment, employed with skill, may be far more useful than a modern system used without regard for operational considerations.

A good example of the importance of tactics is provided by the change in balance between tank and antitank forces during the fighting in the Sinai during the 1973 war. In 1967, Israeli tank units were able to attack and defeat even heavily entrenched Arab infantry units, quickly and with relatively little difficulty. The Egyptians, recognized that Israel's reliance on tanks was a potential weakness, and essentially transformed their infantry into specialized antitank troops. The effectiveness of this is well known: during the opening days of the 1973 fighting, Israeli tanks, operating in much the same fashion as they had in 1967, suffered heavy losses from the previously despised infantry units.

What is often not realized is that within a week the balance began to shift yet again, and by the end of the war the effectiveness of the Egyptian antitank array (though still considerable) was significantly less than it had been only two weeks before. In a matter of days the Israelis were able to neutralize Egyptian antitank weapons largely through employing more effective tactics and by exploiting the weaknesses of the Egyptian weapons. By improving tactical awareness, it was usually possible to detect the antitank missiles, and to use smoke to mask targets, machine-gun and mortar fire to kill the

missile gunners or to upset their aim, and to maneuver to physically dodge or hide from the incoming
missiles. Another part of the Israeli response was to
incorporate tanks, mechanized infantry, and mobile
artillery into combined arms teams that could sup-
press the infantry-based antitank forces. This took
advantage of the weaknesses of the Egyptian infantry, who did not have powerful fortifications to
protect themselves from artillery, mortar, and machine gun fire.

The centrality of tactics and operational methods
has a number of implications for the future
battlefield. First, it is not the individual systems
possessed by one or the other side that matter, but
rather the integration and application of various
weapons in a synergistic fashion.[1] This can make it
possible to compensate for an inferiority in one type
of weapon through careful development of tactics
and operational methods. Similarly, it may be
possible to solve particular problems in multiple
ways, relying on different types of systems.
Antitank defenses can be conducted using tanks, or
infantry antitank weapons, or aircraft, or artillery, or
through a combination of systems, depending on the
particular methods of fighting that best suit a military force. No one approach is necessarily better than
another.

Second, the primacy of tactics and operational
methods places a tremendous burden on the people
who first employ new types of equipment. New
systems may require revised doctrines, especially
when they introduce fundamentally new
capabilities. Accordingly, it will be constantly
necessary to reassess the range of capabilities

1 This subject was discussed in more detail in chapters 3 and
7.

provided by new weapons to determine whether or not changes in tactics or operational methods should be introduced. Similarly, the adoption of new systems by an opponent may force constant tactical innovation to adjust to their new capabilities.

The continuous changes in technology place a premium on innovation and flexiblity. A military force that requires much time to develop new combat methods, or that is not able to improvise under the pressure of battle to meet unexpected contingencies, is at a serious disadvantage and may be left sitting with weapons that they are unable to use effectively.

Neither Israel nor Syria gain any automatic advantage from the primacy of tactics and operational method. The edge will go to the side that is best able to adapt to changing technological realities, and that can meld its responses into a coherent solution. In the past, the military forces of both Israel and its Arab adversaries have been able to make such adjustments.

Nevertheless, there are three aspects of the problem that should work to Israel's advantage in the future:

- Israel has an advantage in the ability to adapt to changed circumstances while under fire. Whereas Arab military forces appear constrained by the repertoire of skills they possess at the start of a war, the Israeli military has shown an ability to recognize its operational weaknesses and mistakes and to make suitable adjustments expeditiously.

- Arab military forces that rely on Soviet support often are constrained by the rigidities of the Soviet style of warfare (although Soviet influence may also correspond with local predilections). This is particularly true for countries like Iraq and Syria.

- The Arab countries that have shown the greatest skill in their tactics and operational methods, and the greatest ability to adapt them to circumstances, are Egypt and Jordan, and neither is likely to participate in the opening stages of an Arab-Israeli War in the immediate future.

The Integration of the Battlefield

It is no longer meaningful to speak of individual weapons. Weapons have become part of integrated platforms that include sensors, remote target designation, computers, countermeasures, and the like. As a result, effectiveness has become dependent on a wide array of supporting devices that have no independent destructive capabilities. Moreover, the effectiveness of individual weapons systems is coming to depend on the extent to which they are tied together, their ability to support one another, and the coordinated support provided by other systems. Weapons not integrated into a coordinated system – unless designated for very specific tasks – will be at a substantial disadvantage.

This integration of the battlefield is made possible through battle management and C^3I (command, control, communications, and intelligence) systems. Battle management involves the coordination of varied assets on a real-time or near real-time basis, whereas C^3I refers to the links that tie a military force together on the battlefield. This involves weapons, intelligence devices, communications systems, and command systems that can absorb information, and securely redistribute and present it promptly in a usable format.

This makes it possible for the individual commander to have at his disposal a data-gathering system that acquires and distributes massive amounts of information obtained from a multiplicity of sources. Thus, the commander of an artillery unit may be able to attack enemy units based on information acquired by artillery-locating radars, ground-surveillance radars, signals-intelligence systems, and cameras mounted on mini-RPVs, none of which may be under his direct control. Similar battle management systems are under development for virtually every branch of the armed forces, if they are not already in service.

Electronic warfare is largely dependent on integration. Data on hostile radars and communications systems gathered by physically separated sensors has to be coordinated to provide a comprehensive and constantly updated view of the electronic battlefield, and the information has to be instantaneously and securely transmitted to electronic warfare devices. Similarly, aircraft, artillery, or other attack systems must be continuously advised of the location of enemy electronic systems that need to be attacked. This is not an easy task, since everything takes place in an environment where information even a few seconds old may be outdated. Experience has shown that it can be done.

Naval warfare has been revolutionized by the development of battle management systems. When tied into a command net, individual ship commanders can "see over-the-horizon," because they have at their disposal detailed information on the location of friendly and enemy forces provided by highly integrated naval command and control systems. Typically, a naval ship will receive by secure communications a constantly updated picture of the naval environment to supplement the view from the ship itself. This picture probably will be created at land-based command centers, which will be receiving a continuous flow of data acquired by radars (mounted on ships, aircraft, and on land), optical surveillance (from aircraft, satellites, and remotely piloted vehicles), signals-intelligence systems (operating on ship, aircraft, and land, and from satellites as well), and sonars (aircraft, ship, and ground-based), as well as from more traditional sources, such as spies. Thus, the seemingly isolated naval vessel will in reality be part of a wide-ranging integrated network.

This will require the close coordination of surface ships, submarines, aircraft, helicopters, and land-based sensors. Thus, ships are likely to minimize use of their own active devices – radars and radios – that might give away their position to an enemy, relying instead on incoming data from less revealing external sources. In the integrated naval battle, it is likely that the system that detects an enemy ship will not be the same one that executes an attack on it. A submarine, sitting quietly in enemy waters, might spot an enemy ship, send the information to a centralized command post, where it will be decided to have a different platform, such as a ship, an aircraft, or another submarine, launch a missile at long ranges to the known location of the target.

The air war in Lebanon in June 1982 provided a vivid indication of the impact of effective battle management. Israel's destruction of the Syrian surface-to-air missile sites was made possible through an integrated air-defense suppression system. Israeli commanders had at their disposal an array of sensors that provided them with detailed coverage of the Syrian air-defense system. They had numerous electronic intelligence systems to monitor the radar and radio signals of Syrian units, supported by mini-RPVs, long-range cameras, and agents on the ground. Using this information, they were able to employ the method that best suited the particular circumstances. Electronic countermeasures could be brought into action, using airborne or ground-based systems, or attacks could be launched by aircraft or artillery against the Syrian air-defense sites.[2]

Clearly Israel has developed considerable skills in the employment of complex battle management systems. There are strong reasons to believe that Israel will exploit the opportunities offered by new technologies to further enhance its capabilities. At the same time, Arab countries also have been taking steps to enhance their command and control capabilities. The Soviet Union has supplied advanced air defense command and control systems to both the Syrians and the Libyans, the United States has provided similar systems to Saudi Arabia, Jordan, and Egypt, and the French have aided Iraq and Kuwait.

The centralization inherent in command and control systems creates vulnerabilities, since a breakdown of any component can result in the collapse of the whole system, immobilizing large parts of a country's order of battle. There is also a danger of the enemy penetrating the command and control system, inserting false or misleading information, or that steps could be taken to jam signals or to destroy critical nodes in the system. Moreover, an enemy can acquire a considerable amount of information from analysis of a command and control system, providing target data needed to attack headquarters or combat units. The Egyptians did this with considerable success during the 1973 war, using radio direction finding to identify and locate

---

[2] S.V. Seroshtan, "Local Wars," *Voyenno-Istoricheskiy Zurnal*, No. 3, 1986, as translated by U.S. Joint Publication Research Service, "Electronic Combat in Local Wars in Near East," UMA-86-047, pp. 69-75, and W. Seth Carus, "Military Lessons of the 1982 Israel-Syria Conflict," pp. 261-270, in Robert Harkavy and Stephanie Neuman, eds., *The Lessons of Recent Wars in the Third World* (Lexington, Mass.: Lexington Books, 1985).

high-value Israeli targets.

The appearance of sophisticated command and control systems in Arab arsenals tends to minimize the edge Israel gains from its own high-quality command and control system. Nevertheless, Israel still retains four significant advantages.

- The Israeli systems tend to be more sophisticated and less vulnerable than those available to Arab countries, as evidenced by the complex coordination that took place in 1982. In general, Israel will have state-of-the-art command and control systems, comparable to some of the best available anywhere, while Arab countries will depend on less capable "export"

- The Israeli systems generally are built locally, whereas Arab countries are dependent on overseas suppliers. Thus, Israel can more easily adapt its own system to new circumstances, is better able to maintain secrecy over the capabilities of its system, and can rely on its own maintenance personnel and its own stocks of readily available spare parts.

- Israel has a significant edge in counter-command and control activities. As was shown in 1982, Israeli capabilities in this respect are quite sophisticated. Although many Arab countries operate sophisticated and effective communications intercept and jamming equipment (often supplied by the Soviet Union), only Egypt appears to have more than rudimentary capabilities.

- Every Arab country has its own national command and control systems, and there is only limited coordination between countries. Although it is possible to develop links between the systems, as demonstrated by Saudi Arabia's ability to transmit AWACS data to Kuwait, it is unlikely that this could be done unless some pre-war preparations were made. This will tend to limit the effectiveness of a spontaneous coordinated strike.

The Continued Importance of the Close-In Battle

Despite the development of deep-strike attack weapons, capable of attacking targets hundreds of miles in the enemy rear, the forward battlefield – the area where the combatants are in direct contact – will remain critical. It will never be possible to destroy all enemy forces before they get to the battlefield, and so it will be necessary to engage and defeat his forces in battles when the two sides are in sight of one another. Moreover, once enemy military forces get close to friendly units, it will be difficult to rely on deep-attack weapons, which may not be able to discriminate between friendly and enemy equipment. Thus, unless an army is able to fight and defeat opposing forces in face-to-face combat, the ability to launch deep strikes will be of limited value.

It will be necessary to provide ground forces with weapons able to defeat even the best protected enemy systems, and at the same time provide maximum protection from enemy weapons. Many traditional weapons, as appropriately modified to the new circumstances, will remain critical. Battle tanks, antitank weapons, mines, mortars, and field artillery will remain, as will the traditional ground-combat arms, armor, infantry, and field artillery. The traditional combat arms will be strengthened through improvements in protection, mobility, lethality, and information gathering.

This will result in an overall upgrading of relative capabilities. Tanks made more vulnerable by new types of antitank weaponry will be provided with better protection. As a result it may no longer be possible to rely on a squad antitank weapon, carried by a single man (like the widely used RPG systems), capable of penetrating the frontal armor of the improved main battle tanks. Instead, crew-served weapons, either infantry-operated antitank missiles or large rocket launchers or high velocity guns (like those carried on tanks) may become necessary.

Because it will still be necessary to retain the traditional arms – infantry, tanks, and artillery – and because of the destructiveness of modern weapons, armies will not be able to easily reduce casualties and a considerable number of soldiers will continue to be exposed to hostile fire on the forward edge of the battlefield.

Potential Increases in Lethality

Weapons are becoming more destructive and more accurate, making them highly lethal. More powerful explosives and new designs have made it possible to make improvements on the standard ammunition of the 1960s and 1970s – including ordinary iron bombs, artillery and mortar shells, and tank ammunition.[3]

Less traditional types of ordnance, like fuel-air explosives, self-forging projectiles, and cluster munitions, can provide even greater increases in lethality. Fuel-air explosives (FAE) create a powerful blast effect from the detonation of fuel dispersed in aerosol form. This blast is so powerful that an FAE weapon can destroy an aircraft protected by 6 feet of concrete. It is estimated that 100% of the infantry within the

---

[3] Examples include the U.S. Air Force's BLU-109/B, a 2,000 pound bomb specially designed to penetrate bunkers, and the Israel Military Industry Hetz (Arrow) armor piercing tank ammunition. On the BLU-109/B, see Mark Hewish, Bill Sweetman, and Gerard Turbe, "Air-to-surface weapons – new technologies for prevision guidance and stand-off delivery," *International Defense Review*, May 1986, pp. 601-602. The Hetz is described in Carus, "Military Lessons of the 1982 Israel-Syria Conflict," p. 270.

central blast-effect area are likely to be killed by an FAE explosion.[4] Self-forging projectiles, also known as explosively-formed fragments, are antitank warheads used in the new generation of "brilliant" submunitions. Such weapons create a high velocity, armor-piercing projectile when the warhead is detonated, increasing the armor penetration of submunitions over what could be achieved by other means.[5]

The improvements in accuracy in recent years have been rapid, and it is expected that this trend will continue. Even without sophisticated terminal guidance systems, it is possible to place ordnance with considerable precision. Modern artillery fire-control systems enable field artillery to attain greater accuracy. Tank fire-control systems make it possible for tanks to engage targets at ranges of 4000 meters. Aircraft weapons-delivery systems have increased the accuracy of conventional iron bombs, and in some cases may approach the accuracy obtained by using smart munitions.[6]

In theory, the increased accuracy and destructiveness of modern ordnance means that a

---

[4] Kenneth Brower, "Fuel-air explosives: a blow to dismounted infantry," *International Defense Review*, October 1987, pp. 1405-1407, and W. Seth Carus, *The Threat to Israel's Air Bases* (Washington D.C.: American Israel Public Affairs Committee, 1985), pp. 52-53.

[5] Ulrich Hornemann, Gustav Adolf Schroder, and Klaus Weimann, "Explosively-formed Projectile Warheads," *Military Technology*, April 1987, pp. 36-51, provide a detailed discussion of the devlopment and employment of such munitions.

[6] Joscelyne Rees, "Precision bombing -- fact or fiction," *Military Technology*, April 1987, pp. 54-64.

smaller number of rounds can achieve a greater result. This is one reason for the increasing pace of battlefield action: advanced ordnance makes it possible to achieve extraordinary destruction in only a very short period of time over greater distances.

Past experience, however, casts some doubt on predictions of reduced ammunition consumption. The large amounts used in the 1973 war surprised most experts, and caused the United States military to significantly increase anticipated consumption rates. In many cases, sophisticated weapons were less reliable than expected. This was clearly evident in the case of anti-aircraft missiles. Although a missile like the SA-6 was thought to have kill-probability in excess of 90%, in actual combat it required 50 to 55 missiles fired for each aircraft destroyed. The discrepancy with the SA-7 was even worse: instead of a kill-probability of 90%, it took 4,350 to destroy two or three aircraft (0.07%). Thus, instead of one missile needed per kill, between 1,500 and 2,200 were fired for every plane destroyed.[7]

At the same time, however, there are many weapons that have performed roughly as expected. Thus, the Sidewinder AIM-9L missile achieved kill rates of 70% in 1982, as used by both the Israelis in Lebanon and the British in the Falklands. The Israeli Air Force had an 88% success rate with the Maverick air-to-ground missile during the 1973 war, and the United States military had a 72% rate in Vietnam. The TOW antitank missile performed equally well during the 1982 Lebanon fighting.[8]

---

[7] Jasjit Singh, *Air Power in Modern Warfare* (New Delhi: Lancer International, 1985), pp. 89-90.

[8] "Maverick's many faces," *Flight International,* March 10, 1984, p. 631.

The effectiveness of weapons, however, depends much on factors other than operational characteristics. Through appropriate operational responses, adoption of countermeasure devices, and use of camouflage, concealment, and deception the effectiveness of most weapons can be substantially degraded. The potential effectiveness of a weapon, therefore, may never be realized if the enemy employs appropriate responses that protect against its destructive effects or that degrade accuracy. Hence, it is not self-evident that weapons will achieve maximum results in battle. This enhances the value of surprise weapons, since by definition an enemy has no prepared responses ready for them, and so the weapon may actually achieve its potential lethality.

Operational Responses: There is some historical evidence to suggest that casualty rates do not necessarily increase when weapons of greater lethality appear. According to one estimate, one hundred years ago it was not unusual for armies to lose between 10 and 20 percent of their strength in a single day, but despite the increasing destructiveness of weapons this had dropped to around 1 to 3 percent by World War II. Loss rates for Israeli forces during the 1973 war were estimated at 1.8% per day.[9] There is a simple explanation for this seeming paradox. As weapons grow more dangerous, armies tend to disperse, reducing the number of their men placed into jeopardy. Thus, increased weapons effectiveness has led to reductions in the density of combat forces

---

[9] See James J. Schneider, "The Theory of the Empty Battlefield," *RUSI Journal for Defence Studies*, September 1987, pp. 37-44, T.N. Dupuy, "History and Modern Battle," *Army*, November 1982, p. 28.

on the battlefield and to increases in unit mobility.[10]

This dispersion changes the character of the battlefield. Armies must be able to control units that are separated physically, and the quality of lower ranking officers must increase. These particular characteristics tend to work to the benefit of armies that encourage initiative, that can operate flexible command and control systems, and that have high quality manpower. In general, these trends tend to favor Israel, and work to the disadvantage of Syria.

Countermeasure Devices: Defending against weapons employing sophisticated guidance systems is increasingly dependent on countermeasure devices and techniques. Indeed, many otherwise potent weapons become totally ineffective in the presence of effective countermeasures that can make so-phisticated systems obsolescent overnight. The countermeasures can be relatively simple, but usu-ally a combination of equipment and tactics is needed. It is likely that the survivability of aircraft faced with modern air defenses, or of warships threatened by modern antiship missiles, will depend primarily on the use of electronic countermeasures (jamming, chaff, decoys, etc.) that can deceive or confuse missile guidance systems.

The combination of tactics and equipment is illustrated by modern air combat. Aircraft rely on electronic countermeasures to jam or decoy the guidance systems of anti-aircraft weapons, as well as appropriate tactics to minimize the threat posed by air defenses, including careful selection of ingress and egress routes and reliance on weapons-release methods that reduce exposure to attack. Similarly,

---

10 William G. Stewart, "Interaction of Firepower, Mobility, and Dispersion," *Military Review*, March 1960, pp. 25-33.

battle tanks now employ reactive and composite armors to defeat shaped-charge warheads, as well as tactics to prevent the enemy from being able to fire antitank weapons effectively.

The measure-countermeasure cycle, therefore, places a premium on surprise, since once a system is known to exist and its characteristics are understood it is usually possible to devise countermeasures that will reduce or even completely negate its effectiveness. Clearly, weapons that can be easily countered should be avoided, especially if the acquisition costs are high, and those against which it is harder to devise countermeasures should be preferred.

The lack of technical and industrial infrastructures will create especially severe problems for Arab military forces in the area of countermeasures. They will be largely dependent on foreign equipment, the general performance parameters of which will be widely known. Although it may be possible to obtain countermeasures equipment from the Soviet Union or Western Europe to use against Israel's American-built systems, it will be harder to counter Israeli-made or modified devices. This will force Arab countries to rely on foreign research and development teams to devise appropriate responses, a process fraught with pitfalls, generally subject to unacceptable delays, and which may result in acquisition of ineffective and less than reliable systems.

Camouflage, Concealment, and, Deception: The ability of modern sensors to locate and identify targets, even at long ranges has made camouflage, concealment, and deception increasingly important.[11]

One method is to reduce the enemy's ability to detect systems by reducing their signature for different sensor systems. The best known example is the "stealth" aircraft currently being developed by the U.S. Air Force. Such systems will become increasingly common in the future. This will result from reductions in the radar cross-section of new systems as well as the employment of infrared masking and a reduction in the use of emitters. Helicopters routinely employ systems to reduce their infrared signature, and ships use sound-damping techniques to reduce the noise they transmit into the sea.

To reduce self-revealing emissions, it will be necessary to increase reliance on passive detection systems or on sensors with low probabilities of being detected. Many active sensors, like radar, can reveal the presence of their own platform, and this may lead to its eventual destruction, especially in view of the proliferation of radar-homing weapons like those used by Israel in 1982. Headquarters are also becoming increasingly vulnerable as they are more tightly connected to integrated command and control systems, since communications transmitters may be vulnerable to identification and attack.

Thus, although active sensors, and especially radar, will continue to be widely used, platforms will need passive missile-detection systems for circumstances when emissions-control prevents the operation of radars.

---

[11] Useful surveys of the subject were given by Jurgen Erbe, "Thought on Camouflage and Deception," Military Technology, September 1987, pp. 85-87, and Friedrich Knorpp, "Camouflage and Deception – A Challenge to Army Armament," Military Technology, September 1987, pp. 88-90.

In addition to reducing observability, it will be necessary to confuse the enemy. Decoys that duplicate the radar, infrared, and visual signature of equipment will become increasingly important on the modern battlefield. In many cases, the decoys will be attacked, diluting the enemy effort and causing him to waste precious ordnance on inexpensive decoys. In some cases decoys will be employed specifically to attract advanced weapons designed to exploit some distinguishing characteristic of a target. Even if the enemy does not attack the decoys, the need to distinguish the fake targets from the real ones will take time, which may be in short supply.

Camouflage and concealment obscurants, like smoke, that can mask vulnerable systems from visual and infrared observation, and radar masking techniques, will be essential to protect high-value targets. It remains difficult to hide systems across the full spectrum of sensors, but masking heat sources is especially problematic. This tends to enhance the importance of infrared sensors, like FLIRs.

Surprise Weapons: There is now an increasing premium on the surprise weapon, a system that is fielded without the enemy's knowledge that imparts significant new capabilities to friendly forces. Surprise weapons confer three main advantages. First, the enemy cannot prepare countermeasures against them in advance, so they are more effective than similar systems that the enemy has anticipated. Second, they can confer a powerful psychological benefit on the user, since the victim of the surprise weapon is often left feeling at the mercy of events beyond his control and can lapse into a fatalistic resignation. Third, they throw the enemy off balance and force him to react rather than take the initiative.

The management of surprise weapons poses continuous problems. On the one hand there is a need to keep them secret, but on the other, excessive secrecy may preclude development of combat methods to exploit capabilities. Inevitably, it is necessary to find an appropriate compromise between too much and too little secrecy, not a simple problem. To a certain degree, the solution will depend upon the extent to which the performance of the surprise weapon is integrated with other systems. To the extent that its characteristics require new tactical and operational methods, it will be necessary to disseminate knowledge of its capabilities and to take them into account in planning and training. Prudent military planners will enter combat assuming that secrecy may have been compromised, and not over-reliant on what it can achieve. Incidentally, using a known weapon in new ways may achieve the same effects as a secret weapon.

The Importance of Electronic Warfare

Success in the electronic arena will be critical on the future battlefield. The dependence of modern military forces on electronic systems is almost absolute. Intelligence gathering systems, including those designed to provide early warning of air attack, depend on sensors that are potentially vulnerable to interference. Most modern weapons also rely on sensors to obtain the high accuracy that makes them so destructive. Command and control systems make extensive use of radio communications nets that can be jammed. Electronic warfare includes both the ability to deny the enemy use of electronic systems, as well as stopping him from interfering with friendly systems.

In the realm of electronic warfare, decisive events can take place very quickly, making speed of reaction extremely important. This is especially important at the lowest levels, where it means that potential threats must be identified and countermeasures employed within seconds or minutes, and becomes acute when multiple threats are faced.

This reality has been evident in air warfare for many years. The effectiveness of aircraft depends heavily on the ability of their electronic warfare equipment to protect them against radar-guided antiaircraft guns and missiles and infrared-guided missiles. This equipment must react automatically, since there is insufficient time for manually-operated systems. Similar developments are also taking place in other areas. The survivability of surface ships depends on their antiship missile defenses, which must come into operation within a few seconds of a missile alert. In all these cases, the survival of a platform may depend on the skill with which the automated detection of hostile weapons, and the responses to them, were programed into the countermeasures devices. In this fashion, the combatant has become dependent on the skill of planning staffs in anticipating threats.

The availability of laser-guided weapons has also to be taken into account. They are used with unpowered glide bombs (like the American Paveway weapons), air-to-surface missiles (like the French AS-30L or the American Laser Maverick), surface-to-air missiles (like the Swedish RBS-70), antitank missiles (like American Hellfire), and antiship missiles (like the Swedish coastal-defense version of the Hellfire). Ships, aircraft, and tanks must now be equipped with detectors to warn of the presence of laser designators and with smoke or other effective counters to laser-beams.[12]

Electronic warfare systems are not only self-protective devices attached to individual weapons. An integrated approach is required that ties together weapons (to destroy enemy electronic systems), sensors (to detect and locate them), centralized countermeasures systems, and self-protection systems. This entails pre-programmed automated command, control and communications networks that can transmit information from systems that collect information to combat units or electronic warfare systems. Also needed is a centralized command facility to allow senior officers to prioritize threats and determine what methods to employ against particular enemy systems. Thus, it must be decided whether to destroy a particular radar, or to rely on jamming. If the radar is to be destroyed, a selection must be made between field artillery, air attack (using either bombs or antiradiation missiles), or kamikaze RPVs. Finally, all of this must take place in near real-time relying on intelligence fusion systems that can integrate the enormous masses of data being collected by the diverse sensors and transform it into intelligible and useful information. As military forces rely increasingly on electronic systems, the need to be able to prosecute electronic warfare also will grow. Those able to control the air waves will gain an edge over their adversary, which may be decisive in some situations.

Israel has a critical advantage over the Arabs in the area of electronic warfare. As shown by its performance in Lebanon in 1982, the Israeli military

---

12 For a discussion of countermeasures against lasers, see C.I. Coleman, "Laser threat warning, a growing need on the modern battlefield," *International Defense Review*, July 1986, pp. 965-967.

maintains state-of-the-art capabilities held in high regard by Soviet and American experts.[13] Arab electronic warfare capabilities vary considerably from country to country. The Egyptians have paid considerable attention to this area, as have the Saudis. Recently, Syria has taken steps to improve its capabilities,[14] but Jordan has consistently neglected to acquire electronic warfare systems.[15]

The Operational Consequences of the New Technolgies

To the extent that the effectiveness of weapons depends on the development of new tactics and methods of operation, or on the combination of individual weapons and devices into complex integrated systems, Israel will be the main beneficiary. Because of the support provided by its technical infrastructure, Israel is much better positioned to integrate equipment to meet its specific local requirements. In contrast, the Arab countries are largely dependent on

---

[13] Carus, "Military Lessons of the 1982 Israel-Syria Conflict," pp. 276-277.

[14] Mi-8 helicopters equipped with jamming devices are the only systems identified, but Israeli sources seem to indicate that other types of equipment have been provided to Syria by the Soviet Union as well. Note the comment in Aharon Levran and Zeev Eytan, *The Middle East Military Balance 1986* (Boulder, Colorado: Westview Press, 1987), p. 178.

[15] "Jordan Girds for Its Future Military, Economic Needs," *Aviation Week & Space Technology*, June 27, 1983, p. 59, notes that Jordan was just beginning to consider acquisition of electronic countermeasures systems for its F-5E and Mirage F-1 fighters, and that it had no interest in anything other than self-protection jammers.

the advice and assistance of foreign countries, which also compromises the secrecy of their systems. Even with the best of intentions, it is impossible for foreign experts to devise optimal systems to meet local requirements, especially in the face of constantly changing conditions.

A direct comparison of the Israeli and Syrian military situation is especially revealing. Neither country has a monopoly on bravery or strategic insight, but the Israelis do have a decided advantage in the operational art of war under the new conditions. The rigid style of the Syrian military, like other armies trained by the Soviet Union, is dependent on systems and methods that are not necessarily appropriate for the battlefield likely to exist in the 1990s. In contrast, Israel can tailor its weapons and tactics to the expected combat environment. In order to cope with the new situation, the Syrians will have to demonstrate an organizational and tactical flexibility that they have never shown in the past. Although there are aspects of the future battlefield that will benefit Syria, including new simple-to-operate weapons, the complexities that will have to be dealt with in integrating new types of systems will stretch the Syrians beyond their capabilities.

9: Regional Stability, Surprise, and Deterrence

Israel will undoubtedly continue to enjoy an absolute military advantage over Syria -- and even a wide constellation of Arab states – during the 1990s. But military superiority is not synonymous with deterrence, due to the critical balance between objectives and costs in the Arab-Israeli context. Even with inferior forces the Syrians by themselves are technically capable of delivering painful blows against Israel.

Regional Stability

Several factors have converged to create the possibility of greater regional stability. These include Syria's unprecedented isolation due to its position on the Iraq-Iran war and the consequent ascendancy of the pro-Western Arab states; unprecedented Israeli strategic cooperation with the United States under the Reagan administration; a shift in the global policies of the Soviet Union towards limiting support for

client states in local conflicts, and a resulting brake
on the generous supply of sophisticated weapons' to
the Syrians evident earlier in the decade; growing
economic constraints in Syria that have affected both
the quality and quantity of the Syrian armed forces,
and, on the other hand, a profound high-technology
industrial shift in Israel that has fostered the
development and integration of sophisticated
weapons into the country's armed forces.

Governments in Israel will have little to gain
from instability, and less to gain from war. Wars, no
matter how successful, undermine Israel, economically, socially, and morally. Given the high casualties likely to result from any confrontation with
Syria, Israel's traditional desire to minimize losses
has taken on new importance. As for the Syrians,
although the net firepower at their disposal has
increased in recent years, the unfavorable
geostrategic environment, coupled with Israel's
increasing exploitation of new military systems, are
diminishing Syria's war-making capacity.

There is always a danger of unintentional war
developing from regional situations, especially given
the continuing instability on the Lebanese border
and the existence of other flash-points in the
Palestinian context. But the new technologies are
creating a situation of mutual deterrence, where
neither Israel nor Syria can derive any benefit from
conflict that will outweigh the cost to be paid.
Moreover, war could erupt if either side made a basic
miscalculation or if there were to be a radical change
in regional and international strategic realities.

Surprise

The danger of surprise is a far more acute problem for Israel than it is for Syria because of Israel's

greater vulnerability to attack. For Syria to achieve even limited objectives by military means in the face of Israeli superiority, it will have to successfully mount a surprise attack. This would find the Israeli military with some 80 per cent of its potential order of battle not mobilized, allowing the Syrians to achieve maximal gains while Israeli forces are at their weakest. Surprise will allow them to exploit the vulnerabilities created by Israel's dependence on an unhindered call-up of reserves; threaten the limited number of military installations that Israel has at its disposal, such as ports, pre-positioning sites and airfields – all of which are within Syrian range; inflict heavy casualties, and force the IDF to fight from the position for which it is least equipped and trained – the defensive.

The ability to achieve surprise will be enhanced considerably in coming years by the proliferation of new generation weapons with increased lethality, range, and accuracy. Surface-to-surface missiles, stand-off air-launched munitions, and long-range artillery weapons will be able to inflict considerable damage on targets deep within enemy territory very quickly. Such deep-strike weapons allow attacks without relying on strike aircraft, which are vulnerable to effective air defenses. At present, there are no active defensive systems against them. Thus, an unprepared enemy, who is unable to mount an effective operational response, will be particularly vulnerable to such systems.

The availability of more destructive weapons will require both countries to improve their early warning capabilities on the one hand and to deploy more effective countermeasures on the other. It will also require substantial investment in passive defenses, such as hardening of airfields and pre-positioning sites, alternative roads, camouflage, civilian shelters and duplication of central means of communication.

The new types of systems will contribute greatly to both intelligence-collection capabilities, making an undetected attack considerably less likely, and the options of responding to an impending attack.

The Syrians have acquired some of the individual components of comprehensive intelligence gathering and battle management systems. But they have yet to integrate these capabilities into their force structure efficiently.

In contrast, it is evident from open sources that Israel has made systematic efforts to establish a complex intelligence network incorporating new sensor systems that provide overlapping, detailed information on activities deep in enemy territory. RPVs and more sophisticated drones already have assumed an important role, coupled with huge investment in electronic sensors and all-weather, day-night, optical means. These have been reinforced by data fusion systems that permit real time – or near real time – integration and analysis of information obtained from numerous sources and the speedy dissemination of this material to the decision-making and operational arms of the defense establishment. These systems, backed by traditional intelligence elements such as the excellent human resources Israel has demonstrated that it has placed in Arab decision-making bureaucracies and the Eastern Bloc, should ensure a warning at least several hours before an attack.

This is especially true because a key component of the current Syrian arsenal, its surface-to-surface missiles, require time to prepare for launch. It typically takes at least 30 minutes to fire a missile after it has reached its launching site. Before that, however, the missile launcher has to move from its protected shelter to the launch site. And, after the political decision to initiate a strike, time is required to transmit the orders down the chain of command.

All these procedures leave tell-tale indicators that make absolute surprise extraordinarily difficult to achieve. It is therefore likely that even in the worst case, Israel would have a warning period of at least 4 to 6 hours.

However, it is more likely that that alert would come 10 to 12 hours before, as happened in 1973, given that the more elements that are involved the greater the number of indicators that can be expected. The new technologies have not reduced the number of elements required to stage an offensive. If the number of elements used during the initial stages of an attack is reduced, the chance of being detected decreases, but less damage will be inflicted.

Knowledge of a coming attack is but one element on a comprehensive response to surprise. In the past, Israel believed that the jobs could be done by the air force alone, since it alone could be maintained constantly at a high level of readiness without requiring excessive manpower. This is no longer true. The increasing effectiveness of Syrian air defenses has made it impossible for Israel to rely exclusively on its aircraft, to neutralize ground-to-ground missile threats and support army units that could be the targets of an initial thrust. While the air force will undoubtedly play a key role in either a pre-emptive or defensive response, more and more the focus of Israeli planning will shift more and more to new-generation weapons. Interest is centering on the development of precision-guided long-range rocket artillery and strike RPVs that make it possible to maintain potent attack forces in constant readiness with relatively limited numbers of people.

In defensive terms, an antitactical ballistic defense missile system would have obvious benefits in protecting Israel, but only as part of a larger system incorporating counter-strike capabilities. It is doubtful that any Israeli military planner will base Israel's responses to surprise totally on an untried, untested defense system that, if only partially effective, will allow a significant enemy advantage in the crucial opening stages of a future war.

As vividly illustrated in 1973, knowledge of an impending attack and possession of the means of countering it are not in themselves a guarantee that surprise cannot be achieved. Ultimately, the decision on how the military should respond to the indicators being received and what means to use is political. New technologies will only be able to help decision-makers by rapidly providing a much more complete and credible picture of enemy activities, but will not relieve them of the responsibility for making correct assessments.

Deterrence

Syria has a theoretical incentive to go to war so long as the costs are perceived as bearable. Its ability to inflict casualties, cause economic dislocations, and undermine Israeli national morale might be enough of a temptation, even if a military defeat will result. To the extent that the Syrians view a war in the context of their long-term struggle against Israel, even a defeat might produce political, diplomatic, economic, or social results that weaken Israel's ultimate ability to survive.

To deter Syria from being tempted by these perceived gains, Israel will continue to emphasize that it will consider even a limited conflict as total war, and that Israel, not Syria, will dictate the limits of that war. This tells the Syrians that even though they may intend a quick and limited campaign for diplomatic or internal reasons, they may be running the risk of the huge cost of an all-out war. The new technologies afford Israel the potential to achieve this goal with less force commitment than in the past, making the threat more credible.

Preemption, perhaps more than any other factor, is an essential element of Israeli deterrence. Futhermore, it is consistent with Israel's doctrine of forcing the enemy into a reactive posture, and thus unable to execute a programmed and coordinated attack, opening the way for Israel to execute the fluid and mobile conflict its forces have been trained and built to conduct. It will be crucial for Israel to convince its allies, primarily the United States, of the justice of a preemptive strike, placing a heavy burden on Israel's intelligence community to quickly provide irrefutable proof of hostile intent. It will also be necessary for Israeli policy-makers to convince the United States that Israeli actions are being taken in the context of an actual Syrian move towards war, and are not a preventive war intended to forestall some hypothetical Syrian attack.

The primary targets of an Israeli preemptive strike will differ from those of the past. The main effort will be devoted to the destruction of Syria's surface-to-surface and surface-to-air missiles, in order to remove the threat to the call-up of Israeli reserves and rendering primary Syrian strategic targets vulnerable to Israeli air attack.

While the new technologies undoubtedly increase Syria's war making capacity, at the same time they serve to actually enhance Israel's deterrence – by raising the level of uncertainty for Syrian planners as to the nature and scope of possible Israeli responses to an attack and, simultaneously, by affording Israel the wherewithal to execute a comprehensive, speedy and pinpoint response. Israel's sophisticated ability to develop, adapt and integrate modern weapons into its armed forces raises the specter for the Syrian's of an enemy able to employ surprise weapons of unknown character that could have a devastating impact.

Traditionally, it has also been important from Israel's point of view to project an ability to act independently of superpower support and external constraints. In the past the Arabs have counted heavily on the international community to pressure Israel into cease-fire arrangements before Israel could deal a decisive blow to Arab forces. The new technologies make it more plausible that Israel could launch a knock-out blow, despite increased dependence on the United States. They afford Israel the technical capacity to strike deeply, quickly and decisively. Replenishment of stocks becomes a less acute problem than in the past when conventional "dumb" munitions had to be expended in enormous quantities, to achieve the same effect as designated munitions. The speed of military responses has accelerated rapidly, while diplomatic processes remain unaltered, strengthening the credibility and viability of this element of Israel's deterrent posture.

Conclusion

Ultimately, stability will result from both military and diplomatic components. Syria's motives for launching an attack will be restrained by Israel's growing military edge while continuation of American-Israeli cooperation and consistency in current Soviet policies, will consolidate the currently propitious situation from Israel's point of view. This will require that Israel maintain a diplomatic posture that will keep the country at peace with Egypt, continue the state of non-belligerency with Jordan, and remain firmly entrenched as a valuable American ally.

Appendix

The new technologies becoming available for military applications are remarkably diverse. Innovations are taking place in such disparate areas as digital computers, radars, infrared systems, display technologies, navigation systems, rocket and aircraft propulsion systems, radar absorbent materials, explosives and propellants, ceramic and composite structural materials, lasers, and fiber optics.

The New Technologies

A central feature of the new military systems is the pervasive role of digital computers. Their performance is often the critical determinant of system effectiveness. As new generations of computers appear, they provide more computing power at lower cost, require less space, consume less electricity, and work with greater reliability. This is making it possible to incorporate capabilities that were previously impossible or excessively expensive.

An example of the far-reaching implications of

the new technologies is provided by fiber optics. Fiber optic cables are flexible glass strands through which laser beams transmit voice communications or digital data. Initially the technology was developed by civilian companies to improve the efficiency of commercial telephone communications (a single fiber-optic cable can transmit far more data than numerous, far larger metal cables), but it has found a great many military uses as well. These cables make it possible to transmit masses of digital data generated by the increased use of computers and electronic sensor systems. The most important military applications of fiber optics, however, have little to do with communications as traditionally understood.[1]

Creative weapons developers recognized that fiber optic systems could be used as part of missile guidance systems. This led to the development of the FOG-M missile, an inexpensive weapon now under development in the United States that carries a television camera used by the launching crew to guide the missile. The television image is transmitted to an operator seated at the (computer-controlled) weapon-control station through a 10-kilometer long fiber optic cable. Use of the fiber optic cable makes it possible to put most of the intelligence of the system on the ground, so that a single missile is relatively inexpensive at about only $20,000. Moreover, since the launching crew can search for targets while the missile is in flight, it is possible to fire the

[1] On military use of fiber optics, see Frederic Quan, "Tactical applications of fiber optics," *Military Technology*, June 1985, pp. 86-91, and James Vernon, "Military Taps Into Optical Fiber," *Defense Electronics*, June 1987, pp. 153-163. The difficulty of tapping fiber optic cables and the ease with which they can be concealed are additional benefits of concern to the military.

missiles from hidden positions behind the front lines. The flexibility and capabilities of this new weapon, made possible by a technology that did not exist 20 years ago, have led some advocates to suggest that it alone could revolutionize the ground battle.[2]

Fiber-optic cables are now being incorporated into towed array sonars, aircraft, warship data lines, and land-based radars, and they are the basis of new types of hydrophones and gyroscopes that have the potential for providing smaller, cheaper, and more reliable replacements for existing equipment. In the short term, fiber optics have enhanced existing equipment through creation of easily-assembled hybrid systems, but in the longer term it will result in the development of innovative new devices. Thus, this one technology is likely to have a profound impact on a wide variety of military systems, sometimes with potentially radical implications.

Most of the systems mentioned have originated in the United States or Western Europe. It is likely that comparable equipment is also being developed by the Soviet Union, but unfortunately virtually no information is available on Soviet advanced technology development programs. It can be assumed, however, that during the next decade the Soviet Union will attempt to field types of equipment comparable to those now being created by NATO countries.

Although the new technologies will eventually lead to the development of new types of systems, in the short run the most common result will be hybrid

---

[2] Roland K. Mar, "FOG-M: Another Army Orphan for the Marines," U.S. Naval Institute *Proceedings*, June 1987, pp. 95-97, and John J. Fialka, "Army Engineer's Anti-Tank Missile Idea Proves Cheap, Reliable -- and Tough to Sell at Pentagon," *Wall Street Journal*, April 30, 1986, p. 64.

systems that incorporate new technologies into old systems. Because of the development time required, new systems designed from the ground up to take advantage of the new technologies will not predominate for a long while. More common will be the upgrading of existing equipment through use of new components.

In the long run, however, totally new types of equipment will begin to appear, and virtually every item now used by soldiers probably will be affected in some fashion. As creative designers discover new possibilities, new systems will dominate the battlefield, but it is hard to predict the forms in which they are likely to appear.

What follows is a brief examination of three types of military systems that will have a significant impact on the future battlefield. It is intended primarily to provide an idea of the possibilities and not to be a comprehensive survey. Among the types of systems not included are command and control systems, aircraft and helicopters, tanks and armored vehicles, most antitank weapons (mines, guns, battlefield missiles, and short-range rockets), camouflage and deception devices, naval systems of all types, electronic warfare, battlefield night vision equipment, personnel protection, small arms, and most forms of field artillery.

Reconnaissance, Surveillance, and Target Acquisition (RSTA)

Accurate, timely information about the enemy can make the difference between victory or defeat. The ability to monitor the activities of enemy forces can reduce vulnerability to surprise attacks, and can also make it possible to employ forces against enemy units more effectively. Although traditional intelligence gathering methods -- espionage, interrogation of prisoners, covert observation, and fighting reconnaissance – will remain important, the enhanced capabilities of new sensors are making technical sources of intelligence more important than ever.[3]

New technologies are already significantly enhancing the quality of existing sensors, and are expected to result in the development of a new generation of even more capable systems in the next few years. As a result, military forces can now rely on an array of sensors, including film and video cameras, infrared cameras, signals intelligence (SIGINT), and various kinds of radar, to provide continuous and up-to-date coverage of enemy forces. The coming decade may see the arrival of new types of sensors, like laser radars, that will provide a new range of capabilities. In addition, alternative collection platforms, like RPVs or tethered balloons, are becoming increasingly common.

Photographic intelligence is a primary source of information about enemy forces. High quality film cameras now being exported by American companies (presumably less capable than those available for U.S. forces) are capable of taking high quality

---

[3] Much of the discussion that follows is based on: Office of Technology Assessment, Congress of the United States, *New Technology for NATO: Implementing Follow-On Forces Attack* (Washington: Government Printing Office, 1987), pp. 143-167. A U.S. Army perspective is given in Joseph D. Tullbane, "RSTA: The Key to Success in Deep Battle," *Signal*, September 1986, pp. 37-40. Reconnaissance, surveillance, and target acquisition all have specific meanings as used in this context: reconnaissance involves the gathering of data about a specific area or activity; surveillance involves the continuous monitoring of a wide area; and target acquisition involves identification of specific targets.

pictures of small objects located as far as 60 miles away. Cameras now under development in the United States (for export) will double that range.[4] At the same time, video cameras (which record images directly on tape, and do not rely on film) are becoming more common. Not only is it quicker and easier to process video images, since no film development laboratories are needed, but the pictures can be transmitted by radio over data links to ground stations so that the images can be viewed as soon as they are acquired, and hard copies can be produced almost immediately. Thus, the information becomes available without having to wait for a reconnaissance aircraft – or RPV – to return from its mission and for the film to be developed.[5]

Supplementing optical cameras, and often replacing them, are infrared (IR) sensors of various kinds. Unlike optical cameras, infrared sensors can be used at night or under conditions of adverse weather. In addition, the ability of infrared detectors to sense the heat generated by tank engines, even after the engine has been turned off for 24 hours, makes it difficult to camouflage or hide tanks. Although

---

[4] "Countries Adopt Airborne Cameras As Alternative to Satellite Systems," *Aviation Week & Space Technology*, September 7, 1987, p. 111. Existing cameras can take pictures with resolutions of 2 feet at ranges of up to 25 miles, while the newer cameras will have a resolution of 5 feet at 120 miles.

[5] Kenneth J. Stein, "Reconnaissance Shifts to Electro-Optical; Film Still Preferred for Highest Quality," *Aviation Week & Space Technology*, September 7, 1987, pp. 111-116. Despite the increased use of video cameras, film cameras will remain in use. Under certain circumstances, especially during daylight in good weather, film still provides better image resolution than video.

infrared systems have existed for years, the newer ones provide better resolutions, cost less, and are smaller than those previously obtainable. This has led to a proliferation of new IR reconnaissance and surveillance devices. Reconnaissance aircraft are often equipped to carry infrared scanners, in addition to their optical film and video cameras, and this is increasingly true for other reconnaissance systems as well. Small forward looking infrared (FLIR) sensors can be fitted into mini-RPVs, like the U.S. Army's Aquila or the U.S. Navy's Pioneer, allowing them to provide round-the-clock, all-weather coverage.[6]

Military radars also are becoming increasingly capable. One American industrialist involved in the development of new radars has noted that "radar technology is entering a period of rapid change that may eclipse everything that has gone before."[7] The development of new components is making it possible to take existing radars and make them smaller, more reliable, and better able to extract useful information.[8] New technologies also are making it possible to develop new kinds of radar. Over-the-Horizon radars now entering service, for example, can detect aircraft at ranges of more than 2,000

---

[6] The widespread availability of IR sensors can be attributed to the development in the United States of so-called Common Modules that made it possible to build different devices using the same basic components, which reduced costs.

[7] Harry B. Smith, "Evolution of Radar Technology," *Signal*, July 1986, p. 46.

[8] Eli Brookner, "Radar trends to the year 2000," *Interavia*, May 1987, pp. 481-486, reviews many of the innovations now taking place.

miles.[9] Of more tactical significance are the bistatic radars now under development, expected to enter service in the 1990s. Bistatic radars permit the physical separation of a radar receiver from the transmitter. Using such a radar, an aircraft need not carry a radar transmitter, since it could rely on signals sent from a transmitter located on the ground. Thus, the plane would not have to emit signals that might give its location away – a necessity if "stealth" aircraft are to be truly hard to find. After all, even if a "stealth" plane is invisible to enemy radars, it will be easily detectable if it has to rely on a radar transmitter.[10]

Improved electronic circuitry and associated computer software has resulted in the development of a new generation of Side-Looking Airborne Radars

---

[9] "The USA builds its OTH-B radar barrier," *Interavia*, April 1987, pp. 334-335. OTH radars bounce high frequency signals off the ionosphere. They need tremendous data processing capabilities: the existing U.S. Air Force East Coast OTH radar employs 28 VAX computers. OTH systems have been built by the United States, the Soviet Union, and Australia. In addition to the U.S. Air Force system, the U.S. Navy has developed the relocatable over-the-horizon radar (ROTHR), which is the only OTH system designed to be moved from one location to another. The U.S. Air Force's AN/FPS-118 radar has a minimum range of 500 nautical miles and a maximum range of 2,000 nautical miles. Because the minimum range of OTH radars is so great, they have limited usefulness in an Arab-Israeli context.

[10] A short discussion of bistatic radars is given in Bill Sweetman, "And now, the stealth-defeating radar!," *Interavia*, April 1987, pp. 331-333. Systems fitted with bistatic radar receivers would not be vulnerable to enemy weapons that home on radar transmitters. Since an enemy can obtain considerable information about the strength and activity of friendly forces by detecting and analyzing radar signals, use of bistatic radars would reduce the amount of information potentially available to the enemy.

(SLAR). SLARs generate radar images of photographic quality, making it possible to spot roads, buildings, and even individual vehicles at ranges of up to 80 miles or more. Modern systems now in service, for example, are able to transmit these images to ground stations located 300 miles away. Although SLARs have been in service for many years, the miniaturization of components has made it possible to build models that are sufficiently small, lightweight, and inexpensive enough to be installed in small RPVs. One RPV-mounted system now under development in the United States can scan a swathe of ground 12 miles wide, and the scan area can be as far as 18 miles from the RPV.[11]

The United States and several European countries have also initiated the development of long range airborne surveillance radars designed to locate low-flying helicopters and vehicles deep in enemy territory. Although these radars rely on existing SLAR technology, they can automatically detect columns of moving vehicles located more than 100 miles away. European systems of this type being developed for adoption in the early 1990s include the French Orchidee and the British ASTOR. The Orchidee, carried in a tactical helicopter, can now track vehicles at ranges of up to 50 miles, but the version to be fielded in the 1990s will have double that range. By then it will be fitted with a data link with a range

---

[11] William B. Scott, "Side-Looking Radars Provide Realistic Images Under Adverse Weather Conditions," *Aviation Week & Space Technology*, September 7, 1987, pp. 93-97; J.C. Naviaux and S.A. Hovanessian, "Tactical Uses of Synthetic-Array Radar," *International Defense Review*, April 1983, pp. 446-450. The most advanced radar of this type now in service is the ASARS II deployed on TR-1 aircraft (versions of the U-2). See Office of Technology Assessment, *New Technology for NATO*, p. 136.

of up to 60 miles, so that the signals can be processed on the ground and then made available to intelligence and field forces. In contrast, the ASTOR (Area Stand-Off Radar), which is currently mounted on a light aircraft, will be used in close coordination with remotely piloted vehicles (RPVs). Once the ASTOR has located possible enemy units, RPVs are to be sent to the area to obtain positive identification using video cameras or infrared sensors.[12]

The United States has adopted a different approach in its Joint Target Acquisition and Reconnaissance Systems (Joint STARS). Mounted in a modified Boeing 707 transport aircraft, this radar is capable of detecting and tracking moving vehicles at ranges of more than 100 miles. Unlike the European systems, however, the information collected will be communicated directly to combat units. In its most sophisticated form, this could involve transmission of targeting information to aircraft and missiles while they are in flight, reducing the time lag between target acquisition and attack to a bare minimum.[13]

------

[12] Jeffrey M. Lenotovitz and Keith F. Mordoff, "Europeans Seek Interoperable Battle Reconnaissance Systems," *Aviation Week & Space Technology*, September 7, 1987, pp. 77-85, discusses European programs. Technically, radars of this type are pulse doppler radars with moving target indicator (MTI) characteristics. This means that they are able to distinguish moving objects from surrounding terrain. The helicopters used by the French Orchidee will normally fly at an altitude of 6,500 to 13,100 feet. The computers used to process the data on the ground use technology remarkably similar to that used in the commercially available Macintosh II personal computers (Motorola 68020 microprocessors, 68881 numeric coprocessors, and about 1 megabyte of memory).

[13] The most detailed information on the Joint STARS is given in Office of Technology Assessment, *New Technology for NATO*, pp. 146-154.

These new radars will supplement the many existing systems now in widespread use. Airborne early-warning aircraft, like the American E-2C or E-3A AWACS, provide radar coverage of air activity over the battlefield and in enemy air space. Operating at altitudes of 30,000 feet, such aircraft provide low altitude coverage at ranges far greater than ground-based radars.[14] Nevertheless, ground-based air search radars will remain in use, although they may be routinely supplemented by radars mounted in tethered balloons to provide some look-down coverage.

Similarly, ground forces will continue to rely on ground surveillance radars (stationed on the ground, on RPVs, or in tethered balloons) to monitor enemy troop movements. Such radars, which are now widely used, can detect individuals or vehicles. In addition to short-range versions intended for use by infantry units, there are longer-range types in which the range is limited more by terrain than by the capabilities of the radar. Thus, the French have a system, the RASIT, that can detect activity at ranges of up to 38 kilometers (individuals at ranges of up to 20 kilometers), but only if mounted in a balloon or on a high spot where the coverage is not masked by hills or other terrain features.[15]

Armies also rely on artillery and mortar location radars to detect and track the location of enemy artillery units. Radars of this type, like the U.S. Army's Firefinder series (TPQ-36 and TPQ-37), are capable of

---

[14] Douglas A. Rekenthaler, "Capabilities and limitations of AEW aircraft," *Military Technology*, May 1985, pp. 16-22, surveys the current state of airborne early warning aircraft.

[15] On the balloon-mounted RASIT, see *Defense Electronics*, June 1984, p. 22.

detecting an artillery shell in flight, and of calculating the location of the firing weapon before the round hits the ground. The most critical components of such radars are the computers and computer software. This shows that incorporating new technologies into existing systems makes it possible to enhance range and accuracy, to decrease the time required to make calculations, and to increase the number of targets that can be tracked. As more powerful computers become available, it should be possible for such radars to create data bases pinpointing the location of hundreds of enemy artillery pieces, and to provide the target location to friendly artillery units in real time via data links.[16]

Computers also are making it possible to deploy increasingly powerful electronic intelligence collection systems. Modern systems of this type are able to detect, identify, and locate enemy transmitters, including radios, jammers and radars. The most sophisticated equipment can accomplish this even when faced with electronically agile radars that periodically change frequencies or that emit only in irregular bursts. The premier example of such a system is the Precision Location Strike System (PLSS) being developed by the United States Air Force for use in Europe. The PLSS is designed to automatically detect, identify, and locate hostile

---

[16] Don Parry, "Weapon locating radars: new solutions for an old problem," *Military Technology*, March 1987, pp. 26-35, reviews the current state of artillery locating radar. Typical of the manner in which an existing radar can incorporate new technologies is the British Cymbeline mortar tracking radar. The Mark 3 version of this radar takes the 1960s vintage Mark 1 and replaces the standard antenna with a phased array antenna, replaces an old electromechanical computer with a digital computer, and provides new displays and input devices.

jamming systems and radars. The PLSS system requires the simultaneous use of three high-flying TR-1 aircraft (versions of the U-2) to carry specialized receivers and antenna. The data from the three aircraft is correlated at ground stations to automatically produce an electronic order of battle of the opposing force. It is uncertain, however, that the PLSS will ever see service, since it has proven difficult to achieve the ambitious goals set for the program, but less capable systems similar in nature are certain to be in widespread use in the coming years.[17]

The new sensor technologies have made it possible to develop highly sophisticated sensor systems at relatively low costs and small in size. This is increasing the potential importance of unmanned aircraft in the RSTA process. Existing remotely piloted vehicles, like the mini-RPVs used by Israel in Lebanon (the Mastiff and Scout), will be replaced by more capable versions of the same size, and they will be supplemented by larger systems with greater capabilities. Light-weight composite materials and small, reliable engines with low fuel consumption have made it possible to build long-endurance RPVs that can remain in the air for extended periods of time, perhaps as long as a week. It may be possible to keep high-altitude RPVs in the air for weeks at a time, using solar energy or microwaves beamed from the ground to power the engines. These RPVs will be fitted with high quality film and video cam-

---

[17] Office of Technology Assessment, *New Technology for NATO*, pp. 154-160. The exact capabilities of the PLSS have never been revealed, but it is claimed that it "has demonstrated a capability to locate and report more such emitters [jammers and radars] per hour with greater accuracy and timeliness than can all other U.S. systems now reporting to Europe combined."

eras, infrared sensors, and electronic listening devices. Some will be fitted with lightweight SLAR
radars for ground surveillance, and it may be possible in the near future to supplement, or in some cases
even replace, existing airborne early-warning aircraft with radars mounted on remotely piloted vehicles. In virtually all cases, the RPVs will be equipped
with data links to transmit the data collected to
ground stations as it is collected.[18]

In addition, satellite intelligence collection has
become increasingly important, even for Third
World countries dependent on commercial systems
like the American LANDSAT and the French SPOT.
As the costs of building capable satellites continues to
decline, it is likely that countries in the Third World
will build their own systems. Within a decade it
may be possible for even Third World countries to
own intelligence satellites that combine multi-spec-
tral video cameras, surveillance radars, and elec-

---

[18] Typical of the new sensors becoming available for RPVs is
the ATARS, which incorporates an infrared sensor, two daylight video cameras, and a data link to transmit the data to
ground stations. Although the U.S. Air Force has often
opposed RPV projects in the past, it plans to acquire 260
ATARS reconnaissance systems for use in RPVs. See John D.
Morocco, "ATARS Competition Spurs Technology Shift From
Photo to Electro-Optic," *Aviation Week & Space Technology*,
September 7, 1987, pp. 71-77.

tronic intercept systems.[19]

A military force with such an array of sensors at its disposal could possibly create a comprehensive, real-time image of the battlefield that will reduce the lag between the time information about enemy forces is gathered and the time it becomes available to combat units. It should also improve the accuracy of attacks. It will be increasingly difficult for enemy troop movements to take place without being detected, and it will be harder for the enemy to conceal units from observation.

For the information acquired by these sensors to be useful, the material must be quickly collated and transmitted to those who need it. Disseminating information to the right people in real time, however, is vastly complicated by the amount of data being gathered by the multiplicity of sensors now in use. The quantity of information now available has become a potential trap. Unless steps are taken to exploit intelligence properly, it can overload recipients with masses of material that cannot be adequately analyzed, causing vital information to get lost in the system.

This problem is further complicated by the need to distribute the information as quickly as possible. In some cases – especially in tactical situations – the time it takes for information to become outdated can be very short. This is also true for electronic intelli-

---

[19] According to an estimate by the Congress of the United States, Office of Technology Assessment, *Commercial Newsgathering from Space*, May 1987, pp. 40-41, a satellite system capable of 5 meter resolutions and able to scan a swath 25 kilometers wide should cost $215-280 million. However, this study also points out that it is possible to gain militarily useful information from commercial satellites, such as the French SPOT and the American LANDSAT, with resolutions of 10 to 30 meters.

gence, since the effectiveness of electronic warfare systems, designed to jam or deceive enemy electronics, depends on the real-time availability of accurate data about enemy signals. For these reasons, the systems needed to exploit sensor data are as important as sensors themselves.

"Brilliant" Weapons

By exploiting new sensors and miniaturized computers it has been possible to develop a new generation of munitions that will be more advanced than the "smart" weapons of the 1960s and 1970s (like laser-guided bombs). "Smart" weapons, required some human involvement in the acquisition and designation of targets but the new generation of so-called "brilliant" weapons will be capable of operating autonomously. Those involved in their development believe that "brilliant" weapons will be able to locate, identify, and attack targets without any human involvement. Indeed, they may be able to discriminate between different types of targets, and to attack only certain kinds of targets, such as tanks rather than trucks. Although the United States has taken the lead in the development of such systems, other countries also have initiated similar programs.

The "brilliant" weapons now being developed in the United States are probably indicative of the general possibilities offered by the new ordnance. Among the American programs are the SADARM, the Sensor Fused Weapon, and the Millimeter Wave Terminally-Guided Submunition. The SADARM and Sensor Fused Weapon both rely on infrared imaging detectors, whereas the Millimeter Wave Terminally-Guided Submunition relies on a millimeter wave radar. What distinguishes these developments is their use of miniaturized sensor systems, whether radar or infrared, and integral computers to analyze the signals to identify targets.

These weapons will be delivered to distant areas by missiles or artillery shells, and once over the battlefield will be able to automatically detect and attack targets of the appropriate type. Thus, it will not be necessary to endanger expensive aircraft, and no warning will be given to targets that they are about to be attacked.

"Brilliant" weapons have not yet entered service and have not been tested in battle conditions, so that it has not yet been proven that they can perform as expected. Some critics have argued that relatively simple countermeasures could be developed to bamboozle them.[20] Further, even advocates agree that development and production could be extremely expensive. Nevertheless, the proliferation of increasingly intelligent "smart" munitions is making it more likely that "brilliant-type" weapons will be encountered on the battlefield, even if not in the forms currently being considered.

Deep-Strike Weapons

The new technologies have significantly enhanced the ability of military forces to conduct accurate, all-weather strikes against targets deep in enemy territory. These improved deep-strike capabilities have emerged from a combination of the growing sophistication of reconnaissance, surveil-

---

[20] The best critique of the new technologies is given in Steven L. Canby, "The Operational Limits of Emerging Technology," *International Defense Review*, June 1985, pp. 875-880.

lance, and target acquisition systems which can locate and identify targets at long ranges and from the
enhanced lethality of appropriate ground-launched
weapons systems. For this reason, during the 1990s it
will no longer be necessary to rely primarily on
manned aircraft for such missions, since ground-
launched weapons and attack drones will be widely
available. At the same time, the effectiveness of
manned aircraft will be enhanced by the availability
of a new generation of precision-guided stand-off
munitions and of "stealth" aircraft designs. Hence,
by the early 1990s, deep-strike attacks will be possible
using aircraft, ground-based rockets and missiles,
and autonomous drones.

Reliance on inertial navigation systems has
made it possible for pilots to accurately locate targets
after flying long distances. Although this is not a
new capability, its importance has grown as a result
of the increased availability of stand-off weapons that
enable the attacking aircraft to launch its strike at a
distance from the target. As a result, aircraft can
execute precision attacks without having to fly into
heavily protected air space. In addition, ordnance
that will become available in the next few years will
carry guided submunitions, like the Skeet,
increasing the number of targets that it will be
possible to destroy per sortie.

The stand-off attack capabilities of the new generation of strike aircraft derives from the introduction
of a second generation of "smart" weapons. Rocket-
powered laser-guided bombs, like the U.S. Navy's
Skipper II, as well as laser-guided missiles, like the
U.S. Marines Corps Laser Maverick and the French
AS-30L, can be employed without the launching
aircraft being exposed to hostile air defenses. Indeed,
in many cases, it may be possible for the weapons to
be released without the launching airman ever
seeing the intended target. Laser-guided weapons

must be illuminated by a laser designator, but this mission can be assigned to an accompanying aircraft (at risk to the aircraft), to a remotely piloted vehicle, to helicopters, or even to special operations units infiltrated behind enemy lines.[21]

Television-guided weapons like the AGM-130, a rocket-powered version of the GBU-15 television-guided glide bomb, can be launched without requiring any exposure of friendly forces. The weapon can be released at a specified distance from the intended target, relying on information obtained from the aircraft's navigation system, and the weapon operator can guide the missile to the target based on the video images being received in the aircraft controlling the missile.[22]

The NATO countries have initiated development of a new generation of powered, aircraft-launched weapons as part of the so-called M-SOW program. Three versions of the system will be developed: a short-range weapon to attack stationary targets, a long-range version to attack stationary targets, and a short-range version to attack mobile targets. All three types would be armed with submunitions of various kinds, like the SADARM. It is expected that the long-range version should be able to hit targets that are as far as 30 kilometers from the launch point, relying

---

[21] T.J. Jackson, "Guided Bombs: Then and Now," *Military Technology*, June 1986, pp. 18-25.

[22] Mark Hewish, Bill Sweetman, and Gerard Turbe, "Air-to-surface weapons – new technologies for prevision guidance and stand-off delivery," *International Defense Review*, May 1986, pp. 600-601.

on inexpensive inertial guidance packages.[23]

New weapons expected to appear in the 1990s may use different guidance techniques. The development of chip sets to create Global Positioning System (GPS) receivers will make it possible to fit missiles with navigation systems that determine their position using signals from orbiting navigation satellites. Similarly, it may be possible to produce inertially-guided weapons more accurate than those now possible by using inexpensive fiber optic gyroscopes of the types now being developed. These techniques will influence weapons that appear in the Middle East during the 1990s.

The weapons of the 1990s will no longer rely solely on high explosive warheads or cluster munitions. Even many existing systems will be modified to carry new types of munitions. Specialized airfield attack ordnance, like the U.S. Air Force's BKEP runway penetrating bomblet, will be available for air base attack. Similarly, "brilliant" submunitions will be employed to attack mobile columns.

In the past, targets in the enemy rear were attacked primarily by air. Artillery had only a limited range, usually less than 30 kilometers, and surface-to-surface missiles were too inaccurate to be effective when conventionally armed. This meant that they were suitable mostly for use as terror weapons directed at cities. The Soviet-supplied Frog and Scud missiles fired against Israel during the 1973 war rarely hit their intended targets and had only a limited military impact. Iraq and Iran have fired large numbers of these missiles against each

---

[23] See, for example, Ezio Bonsignore, "LR-SOM + SR-SOM + LOCPOD = M-SOW (with any luck)," *Military Technology*, March 1987, pp. 18-24.

other, but primarily in terror strikes against civilian targets.[24] Today, however, long-range rocket artillery, ground-launched cruise missiles, and accurate surface-to-surface missiles are now in service and can be used to attack enemy rear areas.

Ground-launched missiles and rockets now in service generally are armed with cluster munitions. Thus, each of the U.S. Army's MLRS rockets carries 644 M-77 submunitions, and the twelve rockets carried on a single launcher have a total of 7,728. Similarly, each of Israel's LAR-160 rockets carries up to 187 M-42 bomblets, and a typical launcher (with 36 rockets) has a total of 6,732 bomblets. These rockets will be able to carry "brilliant" submunitions when they become available. The Phase III MLRS will carry 6 Terminal Guidance Warhead submissiles, for a total of 72 per launcher. In contrast, the LAR-160 will carry 4 sensor fused weapons, like the SADARM or Skeet, for a total of 144 per launcher.[25] The introduction of guided submunitions is expected to significantly enhance the effectiveness of these weapons.

Most of the rocket artillery systems now in use, like the MLRS, have ranges of up to 30 kilometers, and thus are of limited value for deep attacks.

---

[24] W. Seth Carus, "NATO, Israel, and the Tactical Ballistic Missile Challenge," *Policy Focus*, The Washington Institute for Near East Policy, Research Memorandum Number 4, May 1987. See also W. Seth Carus, *The Threat to Israel's Air Bases* (Washington, D.C.: American Israel Public Affairs Committee, 1985), pp. 21-27.

[25] On the MLRS see Wolfgang Flume and Enrico Po, "MLRS: an artillery rocket for NATO," *Military Technology*, February 1985, pp. 15-25. All the MLRS rockets can be fired within one minute. On the LAR-160, see Terry Gander, "Israeli artillery rockets," *Jane's Defence Weekly*, July 7, 1984, pp. 1109-1110.

However, in constrained areas, like those found in the Golan Heights, even weapons with such relatively short ranges can be used to interdict enemy operational movements. Some rocket artillery weapons with significantly longer ranges have been developed. The West Germans started development of a 280mm rocket with a 60 kilometer range in the 1970s, the RS-80, but cancelled the program. The Brazilians have built the 300mm ASTROS II/SS-60, which has a range of 68 kilometers. This rocket has been sold to some armies in the Middle East, including Iraq and possibly Libya. The long range rockets are not as accurate as the shorter-ranged weapons, but they could be quite effective if armed with terminally-guided submunitions. Hence, it is likely that as such submunitions become increasingly available, long range rocket artillery will become more common.

Virtually every country in the region is likely to have such weapons by the early 1990s. Israel will have its MAR-290 and LAR-160, Iraq, Libya, and Saudi Arabia will have the Brazilian Astros II rocket, the Syrians are likely to have the Soviet BM-27, and the Iranians will have the Chinese Type 83. Less common will be the "brilliant" submunitions. Neither the United States nor the Soviet Union are likely to export them to the Middle East, and neither Brazil nor China will be able to make them. However, Israel will be able to make "brilliant" submunitions, and it is likely that such weapons will be in service by the early 1990s.

The rocket artillery systems will be supplemented by tactical ballistic missiles. The Soviet Union has been the leader in the development of such weapons. The Soviet SS-21 battlefield ballistic missile has a range of 80 to 100 kilometers, and is capable of carrying high explosives warheads, cluster munitions, or mines.[26] The SS-21 is considerably more accurate than older Frogs, and probably has an accuracy of less than 200 meters (possibly less), compared with the Frog's 500 or more meters.[27] This missile has been supplied to Syria and possibly to Iraq. American experts believe that the Soviets are working on terminally-guided versions which will be able to achieve accuracies in the 30 to 50 meter range, but it is not known if those versions have been or will be sent to the Middle East.

During the early 1990s a new conventionally-armed tactical ballistic missile, the ATACMS (short for Army Tactical Missile System), will enter service with the U.S. Army. This missile will have a range of more than 100 kilometers and will be fired from the MLRS launcher vehicle. The payload of the ATACMS will be 70% larger than that of the existing Lance tactical ballistic missile, and it will be three times more accurate. Initially, the ATACMS will carry a cluster-bomb warhead, but eventually it will be armed with terminally-guided submunitions. The expected cost of the first 1,000 ATACMS missiles currently planned is expected to be about $1.5 billion, but this apparently includes program support so the actual cost per missile is less than the $1.5 million

---

[26] Earlier reports had placed the range of the missile at 120 kilometers. *Soviet Military Power 1987*, pp. 42, 64, and "Soviet theatre surface-to-surface missiles," *Jane's Defense Review*, November 2, 1985, p. 975. The exact range will depend on the weight of the payload, and the payload weight will vary according to the type of warhead being carried.

[27] CEP (Circular Error Probable) refers to the distance from the intended impact point within which 50% of missiles will fall.

each implied.[28] Although it is unlikely that the United States will export this weapon to the Middle East, it will probably stimulate the development by other countries of similar missiles, which will be acquired by Middle Eastern armies. In essence, it heralds the dawn of a new era in which highly accurate, short range surface-to-surface missiles are accepted elements in the arsenals of all military powers relying on sophisticated munitions.

Other countries are also working on tactical ballistic missiles, including Argentina, Brazil, Egypt, Indonesia, Iraq, Israel, Pakistan, South Korea, Taiwan, Libya, and South Africa.[29] The Brazilians are reportedly developing a medium range tactical ballistic missile. Given Brazil's penchant for exporting arms, this system is almost certain to reach the Middle East.[30] Thus, conventionally armed tactical ballistic missiles will become increasingly common in the coming years, and should be more widely

---

[28] Charles Rabb, "ATACMS Adds Long-Range Punch," *Defense Electronics*, August 1986, pp. 69-75; Tom Donnelly, "LTV Ousts Boeing in Bid War for Army Tactical Missile," *Defense News*, March 31, 1986, p. 22; Tom Donnelly, "Army Allots $1 Billion For Deep strike Missile," *Defense News*, March 10, 1986, pp. 1, 14.

[29] John H. Cushman, Jr., "7 Nations Agree To Limit Export of Big Rockets," *New York Times*, April 17, 1987, p. A1.

[30] Alan Riding, "Brazil's Burgeoning Arms Industry," *New York Times*, November 3, 1985, p. F4.

available than is already the case.[31]

It is not clear that the agreement will successfully limit the proliferation of conventionally-armed ballistic missile systems. First, the Soviet Union, which is not a party to the agreement, has been responsible for the export of the vast majority of weapons of this type now in use. Second, the agreement does not prohibit the export of missiles with a range of less than 300 kilometers, which means that it does not cover weapons like the ATACMS or the Lance. Third, because the agreement is intended to limit the supply and development of nuclear-capable weapons, it is unclear that it will forbid exports intended for use with longer-ranged conventionally-armed weapons. Similarly, Israel has the technology required to manufacture a conventionally-armed tactical ballistic missile: the Jericho II missile could carry a considerable payload at the cost of its relatively long range.

Supplementing the tactical ballistic missiles are new long-range ground-launched cruise missiles. These missiles are basically small, unmanned jet aircraft. The U.S. Navy has developed a conventionally-armed version of its Tomahawk cruise missile. The Tomahawk land attack missile is fitted with a 1,000 pound warhead and has a maximum range of about 900 kilometers. Each costs about $1.4 million. This missile is reported to be extremely accurate,

---

[31] Recently, the United States and six other Western countries negotiated an agreement to prevent the spread of nuclear-capable missiles, including ballistic missiles. In theory, this agreement should reduce the spread of conventionally-armed ballistic missiles as well, since any missile able to accurately deliver a large conventional warhead could also be used to carry nuclear weapons. John H. Cushman, Jr., "7 Nations Agree To Limit Export of Big Rockets," *New York Times*, April 17, 1987, p. A1.

reliable to only a few feet. The United States is continuing development of such systems, and during the 1990s will have accurate versions with ranges of up to 3,000 miles carrying more effective warheads.[32] Although there may be circumstances where such weapons could be highly useful, especially in a strategic context, their cost-effectiveness on the conventional battlefield must be considered dubious at best. A 1,000 pound warhead, even a highly accurate one, will generally not be sufficiently effective to justify such a large expenditure. For reasons of cost, it is unlikely that cruise missiles will appear in the Middle East, even though it has long been believed that Israel is capable of building such a weapon.

A new generation of unmanned aerial vehicles (UAVs) is now entering service, including kamikaze drones. These kamikaze drones are small unmanned aircraft carrying sensors and explosive warheads that are designed to attack enemy systems by crashing into them. They can be launched from aircraft or from the ground, and once in the air operate without human intervention. New systems of this type should enter service with considerable regularity in the next few years.

Kamikaze drones now entering service in the United States have been designed to attack radars and jammers. The Tacit Rainbow developed by Northrop for the U.S. Air Force is an excellent example of this type of weapon.[33] The Tacit Rainbow is a jet-powered

---

[32] Richard Halloran, "U.S. Developing Non-Nuclear Cruise Missile of More Accuracy and Range," *New York Times*, September 14, 1987, p. A12; *Aviation Week & Space Technology*, September 14, 1987, pp. 24-25.

[33] Other examples include the Boeing Seek Spinner, the West German KDAR, and the cancelled Pave Tiger. It is

drone fitted with electronic sensors to detect and locate radars and other electronic emitters, along with a high explosive warhead. Although the initial versions of the Tacit Rainbow are launched from aircraft, it also can be ground-launched. The drone is designed to loiter over the battlefield, until it detects an enemy emitter and goes into attack mode.[34]

Systems like the Tacit Rainbow have many virtues, some not immediately self-evident. Since they can spend extended periods of time over the battlefield, if enemy radars are left off, the drone will merely circle waiting for targets. If radars are turned on, it will attack. Should the enemy realize he is under attack and turn his radar off again, the drone can return to its search pattern. In addition, drones like the Tacit Rainbow can be configured to appear on radar as manned aircraft. Thus, the air defenses are constantly faced with a difficult quandary: if they activate their anti-aircraft weapons they may be attacked by kamikaze drones, but if they do not they may make it possible for a strike aircraft to penetrate into defended air space with no opposition.

Thus, when used in conjunction with other anti-aircraft suppression equipment, drones like the Tacit Rainbow should reduce the effectiveness of air defenses and enhance the survivability of manned aircraft. It should be possible to maintain and launch them using only a few people, and to bring them into action in large numbers in a relatively short

---

likely that other classified projects of this type also exist.

[34] "U.S. Develops Drone to Attack Enemy Emitters," *Aviation Week & Space Technology*, February 23, 1987, p. 26.]

period of time.[35]

Although most of the kamikaze drones now under development are intended for use against radars, preliminary steps are being taken to develop expendable and reusable unmanned aerial vehicles to attack other targets as well. An example of what may be possible is an unmanned bomber program recently initiated by the U.S. Department of Defense. The proposed bomber would use millimeter wave radar and infrared sensors tied to computers running artificial intelligence routines to search for targets within a designated area. Once potential targets have been identified, the aircraft will be able to attack them using intelligent submunitions. Initial development should be completed by 1992. Although it is possible that this particular system may never enter service, it is likely that similar systems will be in use by the mid-to late-1990s.[36]

Israel has devoted considerable resources to the development of RPV-type systems. It was the Israeli Air Force that first demonstrated the effectiveness of air-launched decoys during the 1982 Lebanon War. Using a small number of unpowered Samson decoys carried by F-4E fighters, the Israelis caused the Syrians to activate their air defenses and fire surface-to-air missiles at the decoys. In doing so, the Syrians made it easy for the IAF to identify and attack anti-aircraft positions, and at the same time expended

---

[35] An alternative to the Tacit Rainbow being examined by the U.S. Air Force is the Seek Spinner, which is ground-launched from a container carrying 15 drones. John D. Morocco, "Congressional Pressure Prompts Order to Revive Anti-Radar Drone," *Aviation Week & Space Technology*, August 3, 1987, pp. 84-85.

[36] George Leopold, "Martin Corp. Gets Leg Up on Bomber Program," *Defense News*, October 5, 1987, p. 9.

ready missiles so that they were often unprepared to deal with subsequent air strikes. It was reported at the time that Israel had additional types of RPV systems, including a ground-launched attack drone known as the Delilah. Although nothing has been revealed about this system, its very existence suggests that even in 1982 the Israel military had done considerable work in this area.[37]

---

[37] W. Seth Carus, "Military Lessons of the 1982 Israel-Syria Conflict," pp. 261-280, in Robert Harkavy and Stephanie Neuman, eds., *The Lessons of Recent Wars in the Third World* (Lexington, Mass.: Lexington Books, 1985), pp. 263-267.

Glossary

APC	Armored Personnel Carrier
ARM	Antiradiation Missile
ASTOR	Area Stand-Off Radar
ATACMS	Army Tactical Missile System
ATBM	Antitactical Ballistic Missile
AWACS	Advanced Warning and Communications System
BITE	Built-in Test Equipment
C^3	Communications, Command, and Control
C^3I	Communications, Command, Control, and Intelligence
FAE	Fuel-Air Explosives
FLIR	Forward Looking Infrared Sensor
GPS	Global Positioning System
IAF	Israel Air Force
IDF	Israel Defense Forces

IIR	Imaging Infrared
IR	Infrared Sensor
Joint STARS	Joint Target Acquisition and Reconnaissance System
MTI	Moving Target Indicator
PLSS	Precision Location Strike System
RPG	Rocket Propelled Grenade
RPV	Remotely Piloted Vehicle
RSTA	Reconnaissance, Surveillance, and Target Acquisition
SIGINT	Signals Intelligence
SLAR	Side-Looking Airborne Radars
SPS	Self-Protection System
UAV	Unmanned Aerial Vehicle

Index